Exploring the Southern Appalachian Grassy Balds

EXPLORING THE SOUTHERN

APPALACHIAN GRASSY BALDS
---------------------- A Hiking Guide »

Amy Duernberger

The University of South Carolina Press

© 2017 University of South Carolina

Published by the University of South Carolina Press
Columbia, South Carolina 29208

www.sc.edu/uscpress

Manufactured in the United States of America

Library of Congress Cataloging-in-Publication Data
can be found at http://catalog.loc.gov/.

26 25 24 23 22 21 20 19 18 17
10 9 8 7 6 5 4 3 2 1

ISBN: 978-1-61117-796-1 (hardcover)
ISBN: 978-1-61117-797-8 (ebook)

Contents

Preface - vii

Acknowledgments - ix

Text Abbreviations - xi

PART 1 » ABOUT THE BALDS

CHAPTER 1

Grassy Balds—An Introduction to an Appalachian Wonder - - - - - - 3

CHAPTER 2

Native American Myths and Origin Theories - - - - - - - - - - - - - - - - - 4

CHAPTER 3

Early European Settlement and the Influence of Grazing - - - - - - - 10

CHAPTER 4

Early Twentieth Century to the Present - 16

CHAPTER 5

Flora, Fauna, and a Touch of Canada - 22

CHAPTER 6

Preparing for Your Hike: Safety and Trail Etiquette - - - - - - - - - - - 29

PART 2 » THE HIKES

CHAPTER 7

Introduction to the Hikes - 39

CHAPTER 8

Asheville Area - 41

   Bearwallow Mountain - 41

   Black Balsam Knob - 44

   Craggy Knob at Craggy Gardens - 48

   Max Patch Mountain - 51

   Purchase Knob–Great Smoky Mountains
         National Park and Hemphill Bald - - - - - - - - - - - - - - - - - 55

   Sam Knob - 62

CHAPTER 9

Cherohala Skyway Area - 66

Bob Stratton Bald- 66

Hooper Bald - 70

Huckleberry Knob - 74

Whigg Meadow - 78

CHAPTER 10

Great Smoky Mountains National Park - - - - - - - - - - - - - - - - - 82

Andrews Bald- 82

Gregory Bald- 86

Spence Field - 93

CHAPTER 11

Roan Highlands Area- 98

Hump Mountain - 98

Little Hump Mountain- 104

Round Bald, Jane Bald, and Grassy Ridge Bald - - - - - - - - - 109

CHAPTER 12

Various Locations - 115

Beauty Spot - 115

Mount Rogers- 118

The Lump - 123

APPENDIX A

The Hikes Listed Alphabetically - 127

APPENDIX B

The Hikes by Level of Difficulty- 129

APPENDIX C

Useful Websites - 131

Bibliography- 133

Index - 137

Preface

Once in a great while something happens in your life that is so special that you feel compelled to share and tell others about your experiences. This happened to me when I climbed to my first grassy open summit in the Appalachians. I felt as if I were on top of the world. Rippling blue misty mountain panoramas opened before me. I slowly turned in a circle, like a small child twirling in slow motion, mesmerized with each quarter turn as a new vista came into view. After that first visit to Black Balsam Knob, I became intrigued and then entranced by these mysterious anomalies—southern Appalachian balds! As I began to learn more, I realized that these landscapes are very special ecosystems and that they are quickly falling prey to forest succession. In other words, the forest has been overtaking these open grassy summits for the past eighty years. Not only are the views stunning, but these natural communities are home to unique flora and fauna. I was treated to brilliant bright pink (Catawba) rhododendron blooms cascading over the hillsides in June and blueberries galore in late fall. Some of these mountain balds are home to fabulous flame azaleas. These tree-size azaleas bloom with colors ranging from a soft orange cream to brilliant tangerine and hot red. Those who would never dream of taking "flower" photos find themselves thoroughly engaged.

The origins of the balds are mystery, and scientists have posed various theories over the years. This is another aspect that makes them so special. The more I learned, the more there was to learn—the subject expanded almost exponentially, like a flower slowly unfurling its petals until the complete blossom is revealed. Thus, this book, which initially started as a rather pragmatic hiking guide, became something more. As I continued my research, I began to get a sense of place, history, and time. The southern Appalachian balds have existed for a very long time. They each have their own story to tell. For example, how did Jane Bald get its name? or Gregory? or Spence Field? What is the story of Hooper Bald?

I now have a greater appreciation for these special ecosystems. I also have a greater appreciation for the organizations and individuals that have dedicated themselves to the preservation of our natural and aesthetic resources. The examples of the activities and projects under way to restore and maintain the balds are merely examples, as it is beyond the scope of this guide to provide comprehensive information on all such topics.

Articles and book chapters have been written about these bald mountaintops—grassy or heath covered where trees should exist. The purpose of this book is to share a few of my experiences with you but also, and more important, to offer a brief history of the balds and a description of their current status and to provide a hiking guide to a selection of balds in southern Appalachia—primarily in North Carolina and Tennessee but also in Virginia. I hope that one or more of these hikes will find a place in your heart and that you will be in awe of the beauty of these landscapes as I am.

Acknowledgments

I would like to gratefully acknowledge the following four people, without whom this book would not have come to fruition:

JONATHAN HAUPT, director of the University of South Carolina Press, for believing in the value and concept for the book

NICHOLAS LENZE, a University of South Carolina Honors College student and Honors College Exploration Grant winner, who served as my hiking and research assistant during much of the project. He and I worked collaboratively taking GPS coordinates, notes, and photos; writing trail descriptions; and creating maps. After working with Nicholas for more than a year, I am honored to call him a friend.

WILLIAM LYNN SHIRLEY, who volunteered his time to create the trail maps for this guide on the basis of our GPS trail data. The maps took more time to complete than I had anticipated, and Lynn good naturedly continued to volunteer his time until the work was done.

SUSAN ALEXANDER, Director of Service Learning and Undergraduate Research, University of South Carolina, for believing in the value of the project and for the research support for Nicholas.

In addition, I would like to thank Peter Weigl and Travis Knowles for speaking with me on more than one occasion about the southern Appalachian balds and their continued research on the climate-herbivore hypothesis over the past twenty years.

Finally, I would like to thank the following people, who have taken their time to meet with me to discuss the grassy balds, their ecosystems, and their ongoing restoration and management:

JOHN ODELL, resource management coordinator, Appalachian Trail Conservancy

Acknowledgments

GARY KAUFFMAN, botanist, U.S. Department of Agriculture, Forest Service

SUE CAMERON, biologist, U.S. Fish and Wildlife Service

MARA ALEXANDER, biologist, U.S. Fish and Wildlife Service

JUDY MURRAY, Stewardship Coordinator, Southern Appalachian Conservancy

CHRIS COXEN, ecologist, Southern Appalachian Highlands Conservancy

Abbreviations

AT » Appalachian National Scenic Trail

ATC » Appalachian Trail Conservancy

CMLC » Carolina Mountain Land Conservancy

SAHC » Southern Appalachian Highlands Conservancy

USGS QUAD » U.S. Geological Survey quadrangle
topographic map

PART 1 »
ABOUT THE BALDS

The mountains are calling and I must go.

John Muir, *letter to
Sarah Muir Galloway, 1873*

CHAPTER 1

Grassy Balds—An Introduction to an Appalachian Wonder

I sit on the grassy summit of a southern Appalachian bald with my journal in hand. It's a clear, sparkling June day, and I feel as if I'm on top of the world. The mountains ripple one after another in the distance, and a patchwork quilt of tiny houses lies snuggled in the valley below. These views never fail to inspire me. I am not alone but am joined by others in this high-elevation paradise. A family of four has spread a blanket out on the grass, having a picnic and enjoying the panorama. Catawba rhododendron and flame azaleas create explosions of deep pink and multiple shades of orange within the meadow.

So what are southern Appalachian grassy "balds," and why are they so special? They are defined as areas "of naturally-occurring treeless vegetation located on a well-drained site below the climactic tree line in a predominately forested region" (Mark, 293). In short, grassy balds exist where there should be trees. Their origins and persistence have baffled scientists and captured the imagination of outdoor enthusiasts for years. Hikers of the southern section of the Appalachian Trail have long known the exhilaration of breaking out of the "tunnel" of forest and encountering these high-elevation meadows. Fly to one of the summits in Google Earth and you will see why they were often called "slicks" by early settlers who saw them from the valleys below or from neighboring summits.

What makes the balds so special? At first glance, it's the expansive, often 360-degree vistas that open before you. There is no forest canopy to impede the views. However, there is so much more to the story of the balds. They are unique subalpine ecosystems that have played a role in the ecological, historical, and cultural landscape of southern Appalachia. As one study notes, "Whatever their origin, they are significant sites for rare species, species richness, aesthetics, recreational opportunities and historical value" (White and Sutter, 375). So why are they disappearing after being here for centuries–perhaps millennia?

Native American Myths and Origin Theories

For me, the perfect place to begin exploring the riddle of the wonderful landscapes of the balds is through Native American myths. They are tantalizing and intriguing stories replete with supernatural creatures and giants. Some explain how the balds came to be, while in others high grassy summits are only the settings. Most of the myths are of Cherokee origin and were compiled in the late 1800s by James Mooney, an ethnographer for the Smithsonian Institution's Bureau of American Ethnology.

Perhaps the most widely known tale explaining the creation of the balds is one of terror, heroism, and intercession. It's the story of a monster hornet or bird called the "ulagu." There is some variation in the telling, but in ancient times villages were subjected to raids by this frightening creature. Periodically, the ulagu would swoop down from the sky and snatch a child in its claws, flying away as the villagers looked on helplessly. The Cherokee lived in constant fear as the raids continued and more and more children were taken. Lookouts were sent to the mountaintops, and the ulagu was finally traced to a cave on the sheer side of a cliff. After repeated efforts, the warriors were not able to penetrate the cave, so they made an appeal to the Great Spirit, asking for some way to lure the monster from its den. Hearing their pleas, the Great Spirit sent a terrible thunderstorm to the area, and a lightning bolt tore away the side of the mountain. While the ulagu lay dazed from the lightning strike, the warriors attacked, killing it on the spot. According to the legend, the Great Spirit was so pleased with their bravery that he decreed "that all the highest mountains in their land should be destitute of trees so that they might always have an opportunity of watching the movements of their enemies" (Mooney, 444).

Another origin tale features a slant-eyed giant Judaculla, who lived on top of Tanasee Bald, an area was known as Judaculla Old Fields by early settlers. There were large open fields of perhaps a hundred acres thought to be farmed by the giant. Judaculla (or Jutaculla) is the Anglicized version of Tsul'kǎlû', which means "he has them slanting" and it's been understood to refer to the creature's eyes (444). According to Mooney, the giant had supernatural powers and was considered to be the master of all game animals. Another writer tells the story this way: "On the next mountain top over from Tanasee Bald, Judaculla sat upon his great mountain top judgment seat with a commanding view down upon all of those who may partake in the hunt of his game. The place was later misnamed the Devil's Courthouse due to early American visitor accounts of Judaculla being a type of Devil" (North Carolina Highway Historical Marker Program).

The Judaculla myth and the following story bear a striking resemblance to each other and may represent the morphing of Judaculla into the Anglicized concept of Satan or the Devil. In 1873, the Honorable Thomas L. Clingman (for whom Clingmans Dome was named) wrote that the "Cherokees regard the treeless tracts, at various points on the mountains as being the footprints of Satan, as he stepped from mountain to mountain" (134). He spoke of the Devil's Old Field as being an opening several hundred acres in size on the top of the Balsam Range. According to Clingman, it was more extensive than "his mere footprints" and was his preferred sleeping place (134).

Clingman continued by telling the story of group of Cherokee who met a chilling fate after intruding into the Devil's home: "Once on a hot summer day, a party of irreverent Indians, rambling through the dense forest and rhododendrons, suddenly came to the edge of the open ground, and with their unseemly chattering, woke his majesty from his *siesta*. Being irritated, as people often are when disturbed before their nap is out, he suddenly, in the form of an immense serpent, swallowed fifty of them before they could get back into the thicket. Ever after this sad occurrence, the Cherokees, as sailors say, gave this locality 'a wide berth'" (134).

Interestingly enough, a similar tale is recounted in a work published ten years later. The authors, William Ziegler and Ben Grosscup, wrote that "the Cherokees knew no natural reason why the tops of high mountains should be treeless, but having faith in a personal devil they jumped to the conclusion that the 'bald' spots must be the prints of his horrid feet as he walked with giant strides from peak to peak" (20). The tragic story of the party of warriors who met a gruesome death is also repeated. The summit of Old Field was most certainly meadow-like because the story begins, "On top of the mountain there is a prairie-like tract, almost level, reached by steep slopes covered with thickets of balsam and rhododendron, which seem to garrison the reputed sacred domain" (22).

Leaving the Balsam range behind and moving to the west, we find another intriguing tale about the mysterious appearance of two bald spots near what is now Robbinsville, North Carolina. According to the story recounted by Mooney, the spots were formed when a giant being, with a head blazing like the sun, alighted there and stood looking around for quite some time. When it flew away and people came to look, they found all of the grasses burned from the ground. No one knew what this being was, but "some think it may have been the Sun" (409).

If we travel back east to the Roan Highlands, we find a Catawba tradition rather than a Cherokee one. This myth explains both the bareness of the Roan Mountain summits and the bright crimson and purple flowers of the Catawba rhododendron and is vividly recounted by Charles Lanman in *Adventures in the Wilds of North America,* published in London in 1854. He tells of a series of battles between the Catawba and other Native American tribes that was fought upon the summit of the Roan. The battles were so intense that "the streams of the entire land were red with blood" (205). In the end, the Catawba were victorious, and a number of tribes were exterminated. Accordingly, the Great Spirit caused the forests to "wither from the three peaks of the Roan where the battles had been fought." Regarding the rhododendron, Lanman explains that "the flowers that grow upon the mountain are chiefly of a crimson hue, for they are nourished by the blood of the slain" (205).

While the preceding examples tell of the creation of bald spots, in other stories the grassy islands in the sky are the locations of extraordinary events. For example, Gregory Bald, located in Great Smoky Mountains National Park, was called Tsistu'yĭ, the "rabbit place," because it was believed to be where a rabbit king lived. He was "as large as a deer and all of the little rabbits were subject to him" (Mooney, 407). In ancient times the rabbit king could be seen by humans, but not so in recent history. Another brief tale compiled by Mooney speaks of a Joanna Bald, which was called Diya'hali'yi, the "lizard place," where "a great lizard, with a glistening throat," was frequently seen sunning himself on the rocks (407).

While these examples offer vivid glimpses into early Native America worldviews, they also indicate that many of these places are indeed ancient—possibly predating the arrival of Native Americans and their settlement in the area. As the story of the balds unfolds, you'll see how this element is a key piece of the puzzle. In the meantime, who knows—maybe the giant rabbit king is still ruling the grassy summit of Gregory Bald, just waiting to be seen again!

Supernatural or not, Native American myths provide a natural spring-board to other theories explaining the creation of these subalpine ecosystems. As scientists studied the balds, they researched a variety of factors. Their theories tended to follow one of two paths. In one approach, the balds were considered products of natural forces. In the other, they were viewed as "artifacts" resulting from human intervention or disturbance. The aesthetic, ecological, and recreational appeal of these landscapes was unquestioned. However, by the mid-twentieth century, the overriding question was whether the balds were "natural" persistent ecosystems or were created by human activity.

The theories that cite natural factors for origin are varied and wide ranging. One theory suggests that postglacial climatic changes occurred and that warming and cooling forced both the spruce-fir and the hardwood forests off the mountain tops, leaving a grassy bald. However, after further study, scientists determined that the temperature variations beyond the range within which the trees can survive and thrive don't explain the balds, because the forests would have reclaimed their rightful place rather quickly. While it's quite likely that climatic changes were initial factors, something kept the mountain tops open for centuries.

Exposure to other extreme conditions such as strong winds and insufficient soil moisture has been presented as another hypothesis. Once again, after careful study, scientists determined that these factors do not have enough intensity to limit tree growth to the point of producing persistent grassy balds.

One might quickly consider a series of devastating fires as a possible cause for these ecosystems. Certainly there have been fires that have cleared the forest for a time, but, because of the inherent moisture in the soil, regrowth occurs fairly rapidly. After analyzing these regrowth patterns, scientists have concluded is that no type of fire, unaided, could create a persistent grassy bald.

An insect was proposed as the culprit by one scientist. In 1938, W. A. Gates of Louisiana State University discovered twig gall wasps laying their eggs in oak trees on mountaintops, eventually killing the trees and clearing the forest. He concluded that these insects were responsible for the origin of the grassy balds. However, this didn't explain how balds not surrounded by oak forest could have been created (Mark, 327).

Rejecting the idea that natural causes were responsible for the grassy balds, other researchers supported the concept that the balds were the result of human efforts. B. W. Wells, a botanist at North Carolina State College, studied the grassy balds and, between 1936 and 1956, wrote a series of articles about their origin. Wells studied the grasses and the distribution of a number of bald communities within the southern Appalachians. He noted that these were usually found on gentle slopes on the southern or protected side of a summit. He also noted that a water source was usually nearby. Feeling that natural fire itself could not explain the mystery, he concluded that Native Americans had cleared the slopes and summits for use as long-term camps, game lure areas, or lookout sites (Wells, 17–24). However, since that time, not enough artifacts have been found on the balds to suggest this level of Native American occupation. As researchers continued to study the balds from the 1970s on, they concluded that "there is virtually no archeological evidence to support this possibility (Weigl and Knowles, "Antiquity," 216). Other researchers analyzed the high meadows and concluded that the balds were not ancient but instead were clearings made by early setters for the grazing of their livestock. While this is likely true for some open summits, studies of soil density as well as botanical evidence indicate that many of these ecosystems were in place long before Europeans arrived and settled in the area. However, grazing does appear to be a crucial element in the persistence of the balds.

This final theory returns to the concept of natural forces and is now considered a plausible and compelling explanation. It evokes images of wooly mammoths and mastodons shrouded in high mountain mists slowly making their way across the grassy mountaintops. In 1995, Peter Weigl, professor of biology at Wake Forest University, and Travis W. Knowles, now professor of biology at Francis Marion University, published a groundbreaking article regarding the balds—one in which animals played a crucial role in landscape development. According to the article, many of the grassy balds are indeed ancient. The open, tundra-like areas may go back 18,000 years to a time of receding glaciations. Although glaciation itself did not reach this far south, extremely cold conditions associated with the receding glaciation likely forced the forests from the mountaintops and created the initial open high-elevation grasslands. Then, during the late Pleistocene, very large plant-eating mammals (megaherbivores) roamed these mountains. Their consistent grazing was able to maintain these expansive open areas. At the time, archaeological excavations at Saltville, Virginia (only 60 miles from the Roan Highlands), supported this theory. The fossil record revealed the presence of up to twenty species of large herbivores. These large grazers included the mastodon, mammoth, bison, horse, tapir, musk ox, and ground sloth. According to Weigl and Knowles, grazing by these very large animals lasted until about 10,000 years ago. When the megaherbivores disappeared, smaller but still sizable mammals (bison, elk, and deer) assumed the roles of grazers and browsers, continually maintaining these unique ecosystems for thousands of additional years ("Megaherbivores," 365).

After the arrival of European settlers, the herds of bison and elk were diminished by overhunting. Then the settlers brought their livestock, largely cattle and sheep, up to the lush grassy mountaintops for summer grazing. In such fashion, the balds continued to be consistently grazed until the early twentieth century. Weigl and Knowles stated that "it is likely that, as in many parts of the world, this special natural community is the result of long-term plant-animal interactions and thus worthy of preservation" (365).

Since 1995, when the first article proposing their climate-herbivore hypothesis was published, Weigl and Knowles have continued to research and promote their hypothesis. As recently as 2013, Weigl and Knowles published an article in the journal *Biological Reviews* expanding their hypothesis to additional mountain ranges—the East Carpathian poloninas and the Oregon Coast Range grass balds ("Temperate").

Early European Settlement
and the Influence of Grazing

It is likely that in the past there was an extensive array of open landscapes blanketing the Blue Ridge and that they were larger than those that exist today. In the early part of the twentieth century more than ninety balds in the southern Appalachians were documented by scientists (Weigl and Knowles, "Megaherbivores," 365). Some researchers have stated that the earliest European writings don't speak of open grassy summits and that these meadows were the result of clearing by early settlers. Other writings show that these ecosystems were collectively already well in place when the first Europeans arrived. In this sense, the recorded history is difficult to separate from theories of origin. Both are directly tied to restoration and maintenance policies. Have the grassy balds been around for many centuries, or were they cleared by either Native Americans or early European settlers? This is part of the compelling mystery inherent in the story of the balds.

As would be expected, the earliest descriptions follow patterns of European exploration and settlement west across the Blue Ridge from the coastal colonies. According to Weigl and Knowles, the earliest mention of high-elevation meadows is in the writings of John Lederer in 1669 ("Antiquity," 217). Lederer, a German physician, was the first European to journey into the mountains of Virginia. "Commissioned by Governor William Berkeley to find a way through the Appalachian barrier, Lederer made three expeditions in 1669–70. On the first and third expeditions, he reached the summit of the Blue Ridge and saw the Shenandoah Valley," wrote Harold Malcolm Forbes in the West Virginia Encyclopedia.

Settlement in the mountains occurred gradually, partially because of the rugged terrain and partially because of the extensive presence of Native Americans. One of the earliest clear descriptions of a bald was written by John Strother, a surveyor for the North Carolina–Tennessee boundary survey. On May 8, 1799, he wrote in his diary, "There is no shrubbage grows on the tops of this mountain for several miles, say, 5. The prospects from the Roan Mountain is more conspicuous than any other part of the Appalachian Mtns" (Weigl and Knowles, "Antiquity," 217).

A generation later, in the 1830s, Elisha Mitchell, a prominent figure in North Carolina history, painted an eloquent picture of the Roan Highlands. He wrote, "the top of the Roan may be described as a vast meadow (about 9 miles in length), without a tree to obstruct the prospect: where a person may gallop his horse for a mile or two, with Carolina at his feet on one side, and Tennessee on the other" (Gray, 63). As an educator, geologist, and Presbyterian minister, Mitchell was well qualified to write about the natural world. He is "best known for his measurement of the Black Mountain in the Blue Ridge and his claim that one of its peaks was the highest point in the United States east of the Rocky Mountains" (Documenting the American South). His measurement was subsequently validated, and that mountain was named Mount Mitchell in his honor.

Because the Roan Highlands, even today, provides the largest expanse of existing grassy balds and a variety of significant flora and fauna, it was particularly studied by prominent early botanists, including John Fraser (for whom the Fraser Fir was named), André Michaux, and Asa Gray (for whom the Gray's lily was named). In 1855, another prominent North Carolinian, Thomas L. Clingman, a U.S. senator from North Carolina, utilized delightful imagery as he described the Roan. In a letter to Professor Joseph Henry of the Smithsonian Institution, Clingman wrote, "westward from him stands a victorious rival, the gently undulating prairie of the Roan, stretching out for many a mile in length, until its green and flowery carpet is terminated by a castellated craig—the Bluff" (Clingman, 137).

His descriptions, while more effusive than would be seen insimilar pieces written today, clearly demonstrate his powers of observation and show that he was "quite taken" with the area. Near Mount Mitchell, he wrote of the traveler that "Sometimes he passes through open spots, smooth and green enough to be the dancing grounds of the fairies and anon, he plunges into dense forests of balsam" (137). Clingman continued to evoke a sense of awe: "In the last and largest of the little prairies, one will be apt to pause a while, not only for the sake of the magnificent panorama in the distance, but also because attracted by the gentle beauty of the spot, its grassy waving surface, interspersed with flattened rocky seats, studded in the sunlight with glittering scales of mica" (137).

These early writings not only show an exceptional appreciation for the natural world but also support the idea that, indeed, many of the balds are ancient artifacts. From additional historical records, it is also clear that at the time Europeans arrived, large grazers such as elk and bison were in abundance. As these populations of grazers were hunted and diminished, settlers began to bring their livestock (sheep, cattle, and horses) up to the balds to graze, generally from May through September. Not only were the grasses lush, but also the settlers felt that these high-elevation places were healthier for their livestock. Cattle were susceptible to "milk sickness," which was thought to be tied to the forested areas at lower elevations.

As noted earlier, European settlement of these high mountain areas, especially western North Carolina and eastern Tennessee, occurred gradually. It was not until 1838–39, when the Cherokee were expelled on the Trail of Tears, that the Native American presence was removed. As the area became more heavily populated by settlers, the lowland areas became increasingly prized, the land too valuable to be used as pasturage. Moving livestock up to these high grassy meadows for the summer months allowed corn and other crops to be grown on land that would have otherwise been used as pasture. Also, animals brought up to the mountain meadows did not have to be fenced out of the valuable croplands.

In the mid-1970s, a researcher, Mary Lindsay, was able to interview old-timers about their experiences herding animals up to the grassy summits. A composite description goes something like this: each spring herders would get the word out that these high elevations were ready for grazing. Families would drive small herds (ten to twenty cattle or fifteen to twenty sheep) to ranges that either they or herders owned. Other ranges were leased from lumber companies. Those raising stock for market would have larger herds, perhaps a hundred to two hundred head. The animals were marked with cuts or tattoos on the ears to indicate who owned them. Some also wore bells for identification purposes and to keep herds together. Herders stayed with the animals all summer and charged for caring for them, one or two dollars per head of cattle and less for other kinds of livestock. They put out salt (largely to keep the cattle from straying) and kept the sheep and other livestock together. They were also responsible for disposing of predators that became a nuisance (Lindsay, 5).

Mid-September, as the days began to shorten and nights began to chill, was the time for bringing the livestock down from the mountain meadows. Owners would come and select their animals from the larger herd. The process took several days as the animals were rounded up and put into "gant" lots where food was withheld for several days. It was believed that the lush grasses made the animals a bit bloated and that depriving them of food for a few days would help with the journey down from the summits. This fall "roundup" provided opportunity for a celebration.

According to Lindsay, "This gathering in was evidently almost as much fun as it was work. Even people who had no cattle on the range would come up to help and join in the evening meal of a donated steer roasted by a designated cook and the drinking of moonshine in the evenings. The owners of the stock would often take bushels of chestnuts down to their families" (6).

Descendants of early settlers, while researching family histories, have also uncovered information that confirms this element of pioneer life. Marshall McClung has written several articles about his ancestors, the Hooper family. For example, Hooper Bald was named after Enos Hooper, who, with his wife, moved from Tennessee to Graham County, North Carolina, in 1840. Their landholdings were said to stretch from the present town of Robbinsville to the Unicoi Mountains along the North Carolina-Tennessee state line. McClung noted that "Enos began grazing cattle on the grass of the high mountain meadows including Hooper Bald. They are thought to be the first family to graze cattle in the area" (Mc-Clung, "Hooper Bald"). Also, as ranchers, the family developed a special breed of pony, known as the Hooper pony, for herding cattle."

The same family history also speaks of General Marion Hooper, who was born in 1860. Marion became a "caretaker for the various herds of cattle grazing in the high, lush, meadows. He charged $1.00 per head to look after people's cattle, and is credited with building many of the old wagon roads in Graham County and in nearby sections of Tennessee using only the crude hand tools of the day."

This grazing connection is noted in other writings of the time. In a travel guide published in 1888, the traveler and author Charles Dudley Warner wrote of the Roan, "As soon as we came out upon the southern slope we found great open spaces, covered with succulent grass, and giving excellent pasturage to cattle." What is even more interesting is that he continued thus: "These rich mountain meadows are found at all the heights of this region" (49). This certainly makes one believe that were many of these meadows and that they were natural in origin.

North Carolina and Its Resources, published in 1896 by the North Carolina State Board of Agriculture, speaks of the balds as "natural meadows found on the rounded tops of many of the highest mountains the *balds* themselves being covered with a rich herbage of grass, pasturage to which large herds of domestic animals are annually driven to remain until the return of cold weather" (20).

Another passage, while providing an eloquent description of Roan Mountain, speaks to its utilitarian use as pasturage: "Commanding views, as indescribable as they are numerous, attract and keep the beholder; the top of this most beautiful mountain is 7 miles long, a natural prairie, interspersed with groves, dotted with flowers and shrubbery; it no longer serves merely as a pasture for the flocks and herds of the farmers below, a nobler destiny has been found for it, and travelers swarm over its broad expanse" (293).

The previous passages constitute only a sampling of the early histories, travel guides, and diaries that describe the expansive vistas, the unique flora and fauna, and the use of these open grassy pastures by domestic animals through the early to mid-1900s. From the mountains of western Virginia across the miles to what is now part of Great Smoky Mountains National Park and down into north Georgia, written imagery describing animals grazing in the high-elevation meadows emerged. Later, the images were beautifully captured by photographs showing both sheep and cattle enjoying the luxurious grasses in these islands in the sky.

Sheep on Grassy Ridge in the Roan Highlands—1938.
Courtesy of the Tennessee State Library and Archives

Sheep on Russell Field (near Spence Field) in Great Smoky Mountains
National Park—1930. From the Albert "Dutch" Roth Digital Photograph
Collection, courtesy of Charles Roth and the Great Smoky Mountains
Regional Project, University of Tennessee Libraries

There is so much more that could be included here, most particularly
about the Roan Highlands and the historic Cloudland Hotel, but there are
other works that do an excellent job covering this topic. Also, this guide
does not attempt to document the entire history of southern Appalachia.
That monumental task is better left to historians. However, it is important to note that key events in the region's history such as the Cherokee
Removal, the Civil War, the arrival of the railroad, extensive logging, and
the advent of tourism (especially on the Roan) have played their part in
the early history of the balds. A startling sense of place and time is revealed by unique and sometimes tragic stories associated with individual
balds. Even their very names, both English and Native American, have
their own genealogy. For example, Russell and Spence Fields were named
for early settlers who, according to some sources, cleared these areas for
grazing (Lindsay). (It's also likely these early pioneers expanded naturally
occurring open areas by grazing and clearing.) Gregory, Hooper, Jane,
and Andrews Balds were all named for early settlers, and there are stories
associated with each.

Early Twentieth Century
to the Present

I step out of the dark canopy of forest into the dazzling sunshine, and a vast meadow opens before me. It's early summer, and the carpet of grasses is so thick that I actually sink down a little with each step. I think of the photographs from the early twentieth century showing herds of sheep and cattle flourishing on the lush green grasses. I think of the great changes on the horizon, both socioeconomic and in terms of land pres- ervation, when these photos were taken. Fortunately for us, a series of events occurred that transitioned much of land to "public ownership." These changes brought about our national forests, Great Smoky Moun- tains National Park, and the Appalachian National Scenic Trail, as well as various state forests and parks. The transition protected the forests from rampant logging and other development, preserving the rich biodiversity of the southern Appalachians. Generally speaking, the lands became pub- licly available, providing countless hours of enjoyment and inspiration to sightseers, hikers, backpackers, bird watchers, artists, photographers, and others. The bald summits and the edges between the forest and the grasses (known as the ecotone) have long been known as key habitats for unique and often rare plant and animal species. The irony is that these same events also led to the cessation of grazing on most balds—and graz- ing is now considered a key element in the persistence of these ecosys- tems over time. Today, many balds exist in name only, having succumbed to a process known as forest succession—the gradual replacing of one plant community by another (Forestry-Utah State University).

These events did not occur at a single point in time but unfolded over several decades. The first major development was the establishment of the U.S. Forest Service in 1905 (U.S. Forest Service, "Our History"). Nationwide, it brought large tracts of timber under federal jurisdiction, protection, and management. Along the eastern seaboard, this move came in response to logging by unrestrained clear-cutting, which stripped the hillsides of trees and allowed topsoil to erode into rivers and streams, thus creating a variety of environmental issues. Much of the land within the national forests became available for public use, including hiking, camping, and other recreational activities. However, with this transition to "public" ownership, grazing on these high grassy meadows largely ceased. With the removal of sheep and cattle, blackberry, hawthorn, and additional vegetation began to encroach from all sides.

In 1934, the creation of one of the planet's most richly diverse parks, Great Smoky Mountains National Park, led to a similar set of circumstances. With the land acquisitions and the subsequent development of the Park, grazing within its boundaries ceased (Houk, 68). At that time, there were a number of grassy balds in the Park. Examples include Andrews Bald, Silers Bald, Thunderhead, Spence Field, Russell Field, Gregory Bald, and Parsons Bald. Historically, both Gregory Bald and Andrews Bald were well known as stunning high-elevation hiking destinations. Also, Gregory's hybrid wild azaleas were already famous, spilling a profusion of oranges, reds, creams, and yellows across the summit each year in late June. Park planners wanted to ensure that these particular bald summits were included within the Park. In the years after grazing ceased, succession began to take its toll. By the mid-1970s, observers were concerned about the loss of habitat as the balds were overtaken by successional vegetation. For example, by the mid-1980s, about fifty years after the creation of the Park, the open grassy meadow of Gregory Bald was less than half its originally measured fifteen acres (68). Studies were done, and experiments in restoration and management were conducted. Activities included burning, mowing, hand pruning, and even a grazing project on Gregory Bald (70).The question of whether the balds were naturally occurring or the result of human activity became part of the discussion. Ultimately, policymakers in the mid-1980s made the decision to restore and maintain only Gregory and Andrews Balds—in large part because they were believed to be naturally occurring and historically significant (68).

As efforts to create a national park were under way, another American dream and its realization began to unfold. In 1921, an avid outdoorsman, Benton MacKaye, published an article that launched the movement to build the Appalachian National Scenic Trail—a 2,185-mile-long footpath that would traverse the Appalachian Mountains from Maine to north Georgia. In 1925, the Appalachian Trail Conference (renamed the Appalachian Trail Conservancy, or ATC, in 2005) was created to coordinate the many volunteers needed to make the trail a reality. Determining the path of the Appalachian Trail, commonly known as the AT, involved extensive advocacy and planning, including the incorporation of a number of changes and rerouting over time. As Trail corridors were acquired, the path was routed across high-elevation landscapes in the southern Appalachians. At present, the Trail either crosses or passes very near the summits of at least fifteen balds from Virginia to north Georgia, including several within Great Smoky Mountains National Park. The work of the Conservancy and the dedicated efforts of volunteers have been (and continue to be) crucial to the Trail and to the balds. One example is the volunteer efforts of Stan Murray. In the 1950s, along with performing extensive trail work, he is credited with spearheading the effort to relocate the Trail across Roan Mountain and its neighboring balds (Adkins and ATC, 8). Today hikers along this section of the AT are in awe as the sky opens before them and they are treated to a panorama of mountains rippling one after another in the distance, as well as views of a vast Catawba rhododendron garden on the Roan itself. John Odell, outreach coordinator for the Conservancy, speaks of what is called "tunnel vision"—when someone hikes in the forest canopy for days and feels the exhilaration of breaking out of the "tunnel" onto one of the expansive grassy summits. He noted, "It's no accident that the Appalachian Trail crosses these areas."

As grazing ceased and forest succession quickly began to alter the landscapes, stakeholders began to discuss the status of the grassy balds and their future. From the 1960s through the 1980s, many individuals and entities felt a call to action in recognition of these rapidly disappearing ecosystems. There were also some who believed in nonintervention—in letting "nature take its course." In this scenario, the balds would be completely subsumed within a few decades, and plant and animal species requiring these "open habitats" would disappear as well. This is the point at which a driving question came into play: Were the balds naturally occurring communities perhaps thousands of years old, or were they purely "disturbance" communities, resulting from human intervention? The question spurred much debate.

This was also a time of increasing public awareness of the beauty of the southern Appalachians and the risks of unplanned development and growing concern over the loss of species-rich habitats. Fortunately, several conservation organizations entered the scene and have played a major role in the continuing story of the balds. The Southern Appalachian Highlands Conservancy (SAHC) is one such organization. As an extension of Stan Murray's and the ATC's efforts to re-route the Appalachian Trail across the Roan Highlands, members of the ATC realized that the preservation of just the narrow Appalachian Trail corridor would not be enough to adequately protect the unique ecosystems of the Highlands

(SAHC, "History"). In 1974, this independent land trust, commonly known as SAHC, was formed. Since its inception, the Conservancy has worked in close partnership with the ATC, the U.S. Forest Service, and other federal and state agencies as well as private individuals and groups. For example, in 1982, it assisted the U.S. Forest Service in the acquisition of a 1,387-acre tract on Hump Mountain, thus preserving the land from resort development. In 1992 the organization accepted its first conservation easement—220 acres on Hemphill Bald at Cataloochee Ranch in Haywood County, NC (SAHC, "40th Anniversary Timeline," 16).

In 1980, feeling that call to action, a coalition of stakeholders attended a workshop hosted by the Southern Appalachian Research/Resource Management Cooperative. A variety of agencies and organizations were represented at the meeting, including the National Park Service, the ATC, SAHC, the U.S. Forest Service, the U.S. Fish and Wildlife Service, the North Carolina Nature Conservancy, and institutions of higher education (Saunders, 122–24). Formal papers were presented about the possible origins, the history, and the flora and fauna of the region and about restoration and maintenance efforts (Saunders, 1–6). Attendees explored questions from the philosophical to the pragmatic (Saunders, 101–2). How important was the area's naturalness? How important were the rare species? How important was their history? Should the balds be maintained and, if so, which ones? Should they be restored back to historical boundaries? How should conservationists best go about the process, and what were the economic considerations? How should they go about increasing public awareness? Management options considered included a combination of grazing, fire, cutting, mowing, and herbicides—with grazing being the most effective but not without its issues. However, no single cohesive action plan resulted from the symposium.

Other efforts and activities took place throughout the 1970s and 1980s and continue today, organized by a variety of entities—including the National Park Service, the U.S. Forest Service, the U.S. Fish and Wildlife Service, the ATC, the SAHC, and state agencies in North Carolina, Tennessee, and Virginia. For example, in 1975 wild ponies were introduced to the Grayson Highlands in Virginia to help maintain the grassy meadowlands there. They have flourished and can be seen roaming the Highlands today. In fact, they have become quite the tourist attraction.

An example highlighting the volunteer efforts of an individual is the story of Arch Nichols, who devoted many years to the ATC and the Carolina Mountain Club. According to the writer Leonard M. Adkins, "In the early 1980s, he was instrumental in saving the open, grassy bald of Max

Patch from a developer who wanted to turn it into a resort area. Once the locale was incorporated into national forest land, Nichols, whose age was quite advanced by this time, accompanied fellow enthusiasts in digging the pathway that took the [Appalachian] trail over the open bald, leading to stunning 360-degree views" (Adkins and ATC, 8).

Also, the mission and role of the U.S. Forest Service have evolved since its creation—it is no longer just one of timber management but one of ecosystem management (U.S. Forest Service, "Our History"). For example, within several national forest management plans, grassy balds are recognized as crucial habitats for a variety of migrating bird species as well as for natural communities of diverse flora and fauna. The plans provide structure for the Forest Service's efforts to restore and maintain balds that lie within their jurisdiction. Methods have included mowing, pruning and burning, and leasing the land for grazing. In another example, the North Carolina Wildlife Resources Commission has periodically mowed Little Hump. Beginning in the late 1980s, SAHC has organized hands-on grassy balds management through its volunteer program. It has been able to do so through support grants from the National Forest Foundation, the National Fish and Wildlife Foundation, the Wildlife Conservation Society, Nature Valley, the Appalachian Trail Conservancy, and Constellation Energy (Murray).

Also, an evolution in thinking slowly occurred as many began to believe the balds might indeed be ancient ecosystems created by an animal-contributed dynamic. It was in 1995 that Peter Weigl and Travis W. Knowles published their groundbreaking article regarding the balds, suggesting that animals played a crucial role in landscape development. According to the article, many of the grassy balds were indeed ancient, having been consistently grazed since the late Pleistocene. (The climate-herbivore theory is discussed in Chapter 2.)

In addition to other restoration and management efforts, the Baatany Goat Project has been in place since 2008 on Jane Bald in the Roan Highlands (Baatany Project). Goats are browsers rather than grazers, selectively enjoying woody plants. Canada blackberry is a primary invading plant species, and the goats especially love it! The goats are herded up to the mountain each year in May and graze in movable paddocks until September.

The Baatany Goat Project now has its own website where you can "meet" the goats and the herding dogs so crucial to the project. Accordingly, "the past seven years of the Baatany Project has [sic] first and foremost been an attempt to restore Grassy Bald and Alder Bald on Roan's western balds using goats as an experimental management tool" (Baatany Project). In the summers of 2016 and 2017, for research purposes and with an eye to a pending forest service management plan, the annual herding did not take place. However, the project is still active.

In 2014 the Southern Appalachian Highlands Conservancy celebrated its fortieth anniversary, having protected more than sixty-three thousand acres across its six focus areas, which span ten counties in North Carolina and Tennessee (SAHC, "40th Anniversary," 2). However, the Roan Highlands is its primary focus. According to the SAHC website, "Roan's ecosystem, comprised of 27 rare natural communities, nearly 800 plant species, six federally listed species (spreading avens, Roan Mountain bluet, Blue Ridge goldenrod, rock gnome lichen, Carolina northern flying squirrel and spruce fir moss spider), and over 80 southern Appalachian endemic or regionally rare species, is one of the richest repositories of temperate zone biodiversity on earth.

Roan's globally endangered grassy balds—natural high-elevation mountain meadows—are the most extensive and the highest quality in the southern Appalachians. Its natural Catawba rhododendron gardens are among the largest in the world. Roan's protection is truly a global priority." Another example of the impact of a conservation organization on the future of a grassy bald is demonstrated by the Carolina Mountain Land Conservancy (CMLC), based in Hendersonville, North Carolina. One of its focus areas is Bearwallow Mountain in the Hickory Nut Gorge area near Gerton, North Carolina. CMLC purchased a public right-of-way and in 2011 constructed a public trail to the grassy bald at the summit (CMLC, "Focus Areas"). According to the Conservancy, seven known rare species were protected ("Focus Areas"). Also, the area is rich in diversity—including "meadow and rocky-bald plant communities at its summit as well as significant boulder fields and outcroppings" (CMLC, "Focus Areas"). In addition, the views from three directions are incredible. On a clear day, you can see Mount Pisgah, Mount Mitchell and the Balsams, as well as lovely views down into the valleys below (CMLC, "Hiking Challenge").

The role of volunteers both individually and through organizations has been crucial in keeping invading species at bay. At present, while many of these projects and activities are ongoing, there is no single overreaching plan for the future of the balds. There are, however, ongoing discussions about reintroducing native grazers. For example, there is speculation that elk reintroduced into the Cataloochee Valley of Great Smoky Mountains National Park in 2001 will eventually make their way to bald summits within the Park. Public awareness and support are truly important factors—so perhaps you, the reader, have a role to play in the future of these magnificent landscapes.

Flora, Fauna, and a Touch of Canada

The sun's warming rays pour over my face as I lie, eyes closed, in the open meadow. It is a moment of sublime contentment. My fingertips come to life—gently nuzzling the tufts of soft grasses. I slowly roll over and view the world from ground level, seeing an array of wildflowers mingling with the grasses. I hear the buzz of bees as they make their way from flower to flower. It's the hum of the universe. Thinking about my hike today, I've come to understand that, once again, the story of the balds is more than I initially see, hear, and touch.

« Natural Communities

Regardless of the debate over their origin, naturalists today define grassy balds as distinct natural communities, along with often adjacent rocky outcroppings and spruce-fir forests. What is a natural community? The North Carolina Natural Heritage Program defines it as "a distinct and reoccurring assemblage of populations of plants, animals, bacteria, and fungi naturally associated with each other and their physical environment" (Schafale). Each species is there for its own reasons, but "the plants, animals and other organisms that thrive in the same kind of environment tend to show up together" (Schafale and Blevins, 4). Although the communities won't be exactly the same, there will be a pattern; similar environments having similar communities. They survive and thrive together while pushing other species out.

Even though the animals, fungi, and bacteria are critical members of a natural community, what is usually most readily observable is its vegetation. This is particularly true for grassy balds. These prairies in the sky are dominated by grasses such as mountain oat grass and sedges such as the Pennsylvania sedge (Forest Encyclopedia Network). For those wondering, the Oxford Dictionary Online describes sedge as "a grasslike plant with triangular stems and inconspicuous flowers, growing typically in wet ground."

TABLE 1
Grassy Balds—Representative Plant Species

Mountain oat grass	*Danthonia compressa*	
Pennsylvania sedge	*Carex pensylvanica*	
Wavy hair grass	*Deschampsia flexuosa*	Avenella flexuosa
Dwarf cinquefoil	*Potentilla canadensis*	
Filmy angelica, mountain angelica	*Angelica triquinata*	
Wild strawberry	*Fragaria virginiana*	
Appalachian bluet	*Houstonia serpyllifolia*	
Whorled loosestrife	*Lysimachia quadrifolia*	
Mountain sandwort	*Minuartia groenlandica*	
Three-tooth cinquefoil	*Sibbaldiopsis tridentata*	
Mountain phlox	*Phlox latifolia*	
Catawba rhododendron	*Rhododendron catawbiense*	
Flame azalea	*Rhododendron calendulaceum*	
Allegheny blackberry	*Rubus allegheniensis*	
Highbush blueberry	*Vaccinium corymbosum*	
Fraser fir	*Abies fraseri*	Spruce/fir forest

Sources: Timothy Spira, *Wildflowers and Plant Communities*, 114; S. M. Pearson, "Grassy Balds."

Species of wildflowers flourish in spring, summer, and fall in these open, sunlit environments. Commonly seen are the soft yellows of the dwarf cinquefoil and the whites of wild strawberry and the three-toothed cinquefoil (Spira, 111). The lilac-blue flowers of the mountain phlox, clustering creamy white blooms of mountain angelica, and bright yellows of the skunk goldenrod rise tall above their neighbors in the fall (Spira, 110). The common woody plants you will see are both a blessing and a curse. Blackberries, while often delivering sweet juicy treats, are considered invasives, rapidly encroaching and subsuming the meadow grasses. The Catawba rhododendron and flame azalea are more slowly marching onto the balds. However, their flowering displays are a stunning part of the hiking experience. They also bring thousands of hikers to the high elevations, adding significant tourist dollars to rural economies. Wild blueberries are shrubs that bring abundant berries ripe for the picking in late fall.

A grassy bald is also an excellent place to view the "edge effect"—the biological interactions that take place where the forest and meadow meet (also known as the ecotone). The "edge effect" is a term coined by the conservationist Aldo Leopold in the early twentieth century. He observed that animals (including birds) like to live in areas where they can change their habitats quickly (Brooks, 112). Therefore, these edges are rich in animal diversity. Brooks wrote, "At edges, whether adjoining fields, along roads, or bordering streams, there is a greater variety of food, different types of cover, different light values, and other things, perhaps, of value in the animal's struggle to survive and reproduce its kind" (112). Mammals thrive in the grasses and brushy thickets along the "edges" of the balds. They are key habitats for bird species including the raven, the golden eagle, and migrating songbirds such as the golden-winged warbler, a state and federally listed species.

In considering natural communities, words such as "endemic," "relic," and "disjunct" are frequently used by naturalists. The terms are particularly applicable when talking about a grassy bald. An organism is endemic when it is native to the area. The other terms can be explained within the framework of personal experience.

When I first started hiking these high summits, I was thrilled to leave the sweltering summer heat of Columbia, South Carolina, to be high up on the Blue Ridge Parkway enjoying mild seventy-degree temperatures. I could accomplish this with less than a four-hour drive. However, I came to understand something even more astonishing about many of the plants and animals that make this area their home. Each thousand feet of elevation gain is accompanied by a 3.6 Fahrenheit decrease in tempera-ture (Winegar and Winegar, 16). With that in mind, the day trip from Columbia (elevation 292 feet) to Black Balsam Knob, North Carolina (ele-vation 6,214 feet) is the ecological equivalent of driving more than 1,200 miles from Columbia to the shores of Canada's Hudson Bay. Even today, I find this a staggering thought. How can this be?

During the last ice age, even though glaciation reached only as far south as the Missouri and Ohio Rivers, species of plants and animals re-treated from the advancing cold and ice, making their way into the south-ern Appalachians. As the climate warmed and the ice sheets retreated, these species advanced north again into what is now New England and Canada. However, some species found suitable habitats at high eleva-tions and have remained there over the millennia. These "relic" species are spread out in little fingerlike pockets across the southern Appala-chians. Also, as they spread, they became disconnected (called "disjunct" by botanists) from their sister species to the far north and from one an-other (Houk, 51). One particular example is the spruce-fir forest, a dark, rich, almost mystical community dominated by red spruce and Fraser fir. Spruce-fir forests blanket much of Canada far to the north and also exist in isolated pockets in the southern Appalachians. According to one nat-uralist, "this isolation creates an 'island' effect; and like islands, each of these scattered sections of spruce-fir forest develops its own set of native species. This helps explain why so many species here are rare and en-demic, ones found on these peaks and nowhere else" (Houk, 51).

Although the plants are what one is likely to notice first, these high-elevation ecosystems (including the ecotone) support a rich diversity of wildlife. The U.S. Fish and Wildlife Service explains, "many mammals visit these mountaintops, and some make their homes there year-round. Big brown bats, red squirrels, eastern chipmunks, woodland jumping mice, gray foxes, spotted skunks, bobcats, and black bears have all been spot-ted feeding and taking shelter in these high-elevation systems" (58). Red foxes have also been spotted searching for their next meal—perhaps the southern bog lemming or the cottontail that also frequent the grassy meadows and the forest edges (Houk, 72).

The U.S. Fish and Wildlife Service's brochure continues: "the diversity of bird species here thrills visiting birders, who may be lucky enough to glimpse the rare American peregrine falcon, red crossbill, red-breasted nut-hatch, snow bunting, raven, black throated green warbler, black throated blue warbler, Canada warbler, and magnolia warbler. Many of our high-elevation species are rare, some so rare that they are nearing extinction and are federally listed as endangered or threatened. The Southern spruce-fir forests provide the only remaining habitat for the endangered Carolina northern flying squirrel and sprucefir moss spider" (58).

« At-Risk Species

Collectively speaking, the grassy balds and their adjacent high-elevation ecosystems have long been known and studied for their rich plant and animal diversity. Many species are globally rare and/or federally listed. The loss of these habitats could mean the loss of many of these species. This is ample reason for us to be good stewards of these ecosystems both in terms of management and as we visit and enjoy them. Table 2 presents some of the at-risk species found on the grassy balds or in their adjacent ecosystems.

Table 2
Representative At-Risk Species—Grassy Balds and Adjacent Ecosystems

Plants	
Appalachian gentian	*Gentiana austromontana*
Arctic bent grass	
Bent avens	*Geum geniculatum*
Blue Ridge goldenrod	*Solidago spithamaea*
Blue Ridge St. John's wort	*Hypericum mitchellianum*
Fraser fir	*Abies fraseri*
Gray's lily	*Lilium grayi*
Greenland sandwort, mountain sandwort	*Minuartia groenlandica*
Heller's blazing star	*Liatris helleri L*

Plants

Mountain St. John's wort	*Hypericum graveolens*
Pink-shell azalea	*Rhododendron vaseyi*
Roan Mountain bluet	*Houstonia purpurea* var. *montana*
Roan Mountains rattlesnake root	*Prenanthes roanensis*
Skunk goldenrod	*Solidago glomerata*
Spreading avens	*Geum radiatum*
Wretched sedge	*Carex misera*

Lichens

Rock gnome lichen	*Gymnoderma lineare*

Vertebrates

Carolina northern flying squirrel	*Glaucomys sabrinus coloratus*	Spruce/fir forest
American peregrine falcon	*Falco peregrinus anatum*	
Pygmy salamander	*Desmognathus wrighti*	Spruce/fir forest
Red crossbill (southern Appalachian)	*Loxia curvirostra*	
Northern saw-whet owl	*Aegolius acadicus*	Spruce/fir forest
Southern rock vole	*Microtus chrotorrhinus carolinensis*	

Vertebrates

Virginia big-eared bat	*Corynorhinus townsendii virginianus*
Golden-winged warbler	*Vermivora chrysoptera*
Vesper sparrow	*Pooecetes gramineus*
Black-capped chickadee	*Poecile atricapillus*

Invertebrates

Spruce-fir moss spider	*Microhexura montivaga*	Spruce/fir forest

Sources: U.S. Fish and Wildlife Service, *Tennessee's High-elevation Ecosystems,* https://www.fws.gov/Asheville/pdfs/TNhighelevation.pdf; Chris Coxen, ecologist, Southern Appalachian Highlands Conservancy, personal interview; U.S. Fish and Wildlife Service, Environmental Conservation Online System—Tennessee, http://ecos.fws.gov/tess_public/reports/species -listed-by-state-report?state=TN&status=listed; Protected Wildlife Species of North Carolina, http://www.ncwildlife.org/Portals/0/Conserving/ documents/protected_species.pdf; North Carolina Wildlife Action Plan, http://www.ncwildlife.org/Plan.aspx; Great Smoky Mountains National Park, Threatened and Endangered Species, http://www.nps.gov/grsm/ naturescience/te-species.htm.

CHAPTER 6

Preparing for Your Hike:
Trail Safety and Etiquette

To ensure that you have enjoyable and safe hiking experiences, a bit of planning and knowledge are necessary. The season (spring, summer, fall or winter), the weather conditions, and the length of your hike are elements to consider as you plan your hike. It is advisable always to hike with another person. If you do choose to hike alone, let a friend or family member know where you are going and when you expect to return.

What to Bring on Your Hike »

For a shorter hike, less than one-half mile, you may need to bring only your camera, water and a snack. The longer the hike, the more useful and important the following items become:

- Hiking boots—ankle high (if they are new, be sure to break them in first).
- High-quality hiking socks.
- Day pack—make sure you have a specific place for your car keys and wallet.
- Water—at least 32 ounces and more for longer hikes.
- Lunch and snacks.
- Plastic baggie for taking out any kind of trash, including used toilet tissue.
- Tissue.
- Small first-aid kit (adhesive strips, antibiotic cream, gauze pads, moleskin, and scissors).

- Insect repellent.

- Sunglasses, sunscreen, and hat.

- Headlamp—even if it is a day hike.

- Rain jacket (no matter what the weather forecast is).

- Map/hiking guide (and know how to read it).

- Layered clothing. Even if you begin your hike in shorts and t-shirt, you will likely need a fleece jacket or sweatshirt at the summit; avoid cotton, which holds moisture in when wet and opt for synthetic fabrics, wool, or acrylic blends.

- For enjoyment—camera, wildflower guide, binoculars.

A little bit of knowledge can go a long way to alleviate any concerns you have about venturing into the great outdoors. Reading and remembering the following points can help you feel confident that you will have a safe and enjoyable hiking experience.

« Weather

Because the hikes discussed in this book are high-elevation hikes (most reach more than 4,000 feet of elevation), weather conditions may change quickly. With adequate knowledge and preparation, you can minimize weather-related issues. Check the weather forecast prior to your hike. As discussed previously, the temperatures at high elevations will be considerably cooler (even in summer) than those at lower elevations, where the trail may actually begin. Weather can change, bringing wet, windy, chilly, or cold conditions. If you get cold and wet, you run the risk of hypothermia, a condition where your body fails to maintain its core temperature. The best approach to hypothermia is prevention:

- Stay dry—do not wear cotton clothing, which remains cold when wet.

- Keep hydrated—drinking lots of liquid.

- Recognize the beginning signs of hypothermia— uncontrollable shivering and, later, slurred speech and a stumbling gait.

Another weather-related concern is lightning. It is not unusual for afternoon thunderstorms to crop up, particularly in the summer months. Although lightning strikes are rare, an open ridgeline is not where you want to be during a thunderstorm! If you see a storm approaching:

- Immediately leave exposed areas (the open grassy summits). Lightning activity may be closer than you realize.

- Then avoid the tallest trees, solitary boulders, and rocky overhangs. Take shelter in a group of smaller trees or in the forest.

- Avoid clearings.

- If caught in the open, crouch down on a pad or roll into a ball. Disperse group members, so that not everyone can be struck by a single bolt. Do not hold a potential lightning rod, such as a metal hiking pole (Appalachian Trail Conservancy).

Bears »

One naturally thinks of black bears when hiking in the southern Appalachians—especially Great Smoky Mountains National Park. Bear sightings and attacks are actually relatively rare. Although not naturally aggressive, bears are wild animals, and their behavior can be unpredictable. Treat all bear encounters with extreme caution. What to do if you see a bear? The National Park Service recommends:

- If you see a bear from a distance, enjoy your viewing opportunity, but . . .

- Do not approach the bear. Do not get closer than fifty yards or any distance that changes/disturbs the bear's behavior.

- Do not feed the bear.

- If the bear changes its behavior—swatting the ground, blowing, slapping vegetation—then you are in the animal's space. You are being warned that you are too close. If this occurs, slowly back away, increasing distance between you and the bear.

- If the bear approaches you without these "bluff" behaviors, then move away, changing you direction. The bear may move by you.

- If the bear continues its approach, then try to make yourself bigger and more dominant by standing on higher ground, shouting, raising your arms, and throwing rocks. You want to establish dominance over the animal. Do not run.

- If that fails and the bear makes contact, it may only be after your food. Separate yourself from your food.

- If the bear shows no interest in your food but continues contact, then fight back aggressively. Do not play dead.

« Snakes

Because you are in nature, you may encounter a snake while hiking—but most are nonpoisonous and are just as afraid of you as you are of them. Do not kill them—just give them berth and they will slide away. Only two snakes are poisonous—the timber rattlesnake and the copperhead. Fortunately, lethal snake bites are a rare occurrence. To minimize the possibility of being bitten by a snake:

- Stay on maintained trails and watch where you step.
- Don't reach blindly behind logs and rocks.
- Inspect where you plan to sit when you take a break.
- Wear ankle-high boots for protection.

« Hornets and Yellow Jackets

Being attacked by hornets or yellow jackets is, at the least, very painful and, for those who are allergic to bee venom, possibly lethal. Hornets' nests tend to hang from trees. If you see one, it may be tempting to try to inspect it or knock it down. Just leave it alone. Yellow jackets are more of a concern because they frequently build their nests in holes in the ground near or directly on the trail. Their nests are hidden from sight until it's too late. Yellow jackets are easily agitated in late summer and early fall. Normally the lead person on the trail escapes their wrath. The vibration of the leader walking by agitates the yellow jackets, and they come swarming from the ground, attacking others. If you suspect you are allergic to bee venom, have your physician prescribe an epinephrine pen. Carry it with you, know how to use it, and also show your companions how to use it.

Poison Ivy »

Poison ivy, poison oak, and poison sumac are all found in the southern Appalachians. These plants produce an oil called urushiol when bruised or damaged. Skin contact with this oil can produce an itchy red rash with bumps or blisters. Fortunately, all three of these plants typically don't grow above 3,000 feet. However, you may see them on the trail to a grassy bald. The best defense is to learn to identify the plants. The old saying "leaves of three, let it be" is well worth remembering for poison ivy and poison oak. Poison sumac is more like a woody shrub, with stems with seven to thirteen leaves arranged in pairs. Poison ivy is the most common of the three and is typically seen as a vine growing on trees or along the ground. It has three shiny green leaves emanating from a single stalk in summer, and these leaves turn red in late fall. If you think you have come into contact with the oil from one of these plants, wash with an oilfree soap (or degreasing detergent) and water as soon as you can. Remember that the oil can also get on your clothing and transfer to your skin.

TIPS »

- Learn to recognize these plants.
- Stay on maintained trails.
- Wear hiking pants instead of shorts. They can protect your legs from the rash-producing oil if you brush up against one of these plants (Centers for Disease Control and Prevention).

Trail Etiquette »

Many outdoor guides and organizations adhere to the Leave No Trace Seven Principles developed by the Center for Outdoor Ethics. The principles are:

Plan Ahead and Prepare

Travel and Camp on Durable Surfaces

Dispose of Waste Properly

Leave What You Find

Minimize Campfire Impacts

Respect Wildlife

Be Considerate of Other Visitors

The Center encourages the use and publication of the Leave No Trace Seven Principles, including the following copyright language: (c) Leave No Trace Center for Outdoor Ethics: www.LNT.org.

In short:

- Pack out what you pack in—including toilet paper.
- Stay on the trail to help protect sensitive ecosystems.
- When hiking in a large group, spread out across the bald to lessen your impact.
- Do not attempt to remove plants. The flora and fauna are very sensitive to their local environments and will not likely survive a removal.
- If you are hiking with your dog, keep the animal on a leash at all times. This is for your dog's protection and the protection of others. Remember, dogs are not allowed on the trails in Great Smoky Mountains National Park.
- Be respectful of others you meet along the trail.

PART 2 »
THE HIKES

In every walk with Nature
one receives far more than he seeks.

John Muir, *Steep Trails*

CHAPTER 7

Introduction to the Hikes

The hikes included in this guide have been carefully selected, each for the unique experience it offers. From grassy meadows opening to meet the sky, to stunning 360-degree views, to glimpses of wild ponies, each hike has its own gifts to offer. There are gardens of flame azaleas and rhododendron, wooded glades, and blueberry fields, as well as birds and other animals that inhabit these ecosystems. The seasons create even greater variety—with the bright green grasses of summer changing to the tawny browns of fall and winter. Abundant wildflowers cycle through their seasons, displaying blooms in a wide spectrum of colors—soft creamy yellows, vibrant pinks and purples, reds, bright yellows, and varied shades of orange and white. The flowers of early spring are replaced by those of high summer, and then fall flowers bloom as the days shorten, temperatures drop, and the nights begin to chill.

The hikes are of varying lengths and difficulty, from short, easy walks to ten-plus miles of climbing. The trails range from easy to strenuous, providing a wide range of opportunities to experience the wonder that is the balds. You can easily select the most appropriate hike or hikes by consulting Appendix B. where the hikes are listed in order of difficulty. I have considered the steepness of the trail, the trail conditions, and the overall length of the hike when determining difficulty.

Hiking times, as well as difficulty level, are somewhat subjective. When I'm on the trail with certain friends, I'm always the "donkey's tail"—stopping along the way to take photos, inspect plants, take in the view, or have a snack. When I'm with others, I've been called a "mountain goat" perceived to be scampering up the trail! The times included here are intended to assist you when planning your hike—but travel times are relative. I encourage you to plan for time to enjoy the journey and the experience of the entire hike, not just the summits.

The hikes are organized largely by geographical area, so that you can more easily plan hikes located near one another. Consult appendix A to see the hikes listed alphabetically. Also, for some hikes there are multiple ways to reach the summit. The trail instructions included here provide the most commonly used routing.

In addition, some hikes included in this book are waypoints (or near waypoints) on that wonderful American treasure, the Appalachian Trail. However, they are included in this work as day hikes to grassy balds from specific parking areas and trailheads. Should you wish to experience even longer hikes or backpacking, you can certainly string together certain hikes for a longer hike or an overnight experience. You should check with the appropriate managing entity listed for each hike for additional details.

Nicholas Lenze and me as we began data collection for the hikes—Andrews Bald. Unless otherwise noted, all photographs were taken by the author.

CHAPTER 8

Asheville Area

Bearwallow Mountain »

The hike to the summit of Bearwallow Mountain is one of my favorite "juice worth the squeeze" hikes. At 4,232 feet, Bearwallow is the highest peak in the Bearwallow Highlands (CMLC, "Hiking Challenge"). Located in the Hickory Nut Gorge area, it is only a short drive from Lake Lure, Hendersonville, or Asheville. If you have only a few hours free and are looking for a mountaintop viewing experience, this is the perfect hike! Much of the elevation is accomplished by the five-mile winding drive up the mountain. Views from Bearwallow Mountain Road are already astounding before you even leave your car!

The mountain is privately owned, but in 2009 the Carolina Mountain Land Conservancy acquired a conservation easement that included the summit, protecting it from further development. At the rusted gate

Bearwallow Mountain

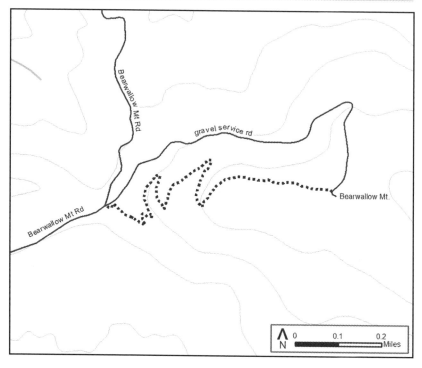

Bearwallow Mountain

marking the trailhead there is now a beautifully constructed trail created by the Carolina Mountain Land Conservancy and additional volunteers, with financial support from other sponsors (CMLC, "Hiking Challenge").

Through a series of nicely built steps and switchbacks, the trail ascends to the summit. In early spring, a garden of trillium appears near the beginning of the trail, and mayapple also covers the hillsides. Numerous additional wildflowers abound. Also, mountain laurel and flame azaleas burst into bloom in May.

There is a gravel service road leading to the summit from the gate at the trailhead if you do not wish to take the trail.

« HISTORICAL NOTE

There is a historic North Carolina Forest Service fire tower at the summit. Although it is no longer used to spot fires, it remained in service until the mid-1990s.

There is also a series of communication towers near the fire tower. Fortunately, the towers do not affect the views and the expansive mountain meadow.

HIGHLIGHTS »

DISTANCE	»	2.0 miles
ASCENT	»	537 feet
ELEVATION START	»	3,695 feet
DIFFICULTY	»	Moderate
HIKING TIME	»	1.5 hours
USGS QUAD	»	Bear Wallow
MANAGED BY	»	Privately owned, but the Carolina Mountain Land Conservancy maintains a conservation easement that includes the trail and the summit
FACILITIES AND FEES	»	None

GETTING THERE »

From I-26 at Hendersonville, North Carolina, take exit 49 (U.S. Hwy 64) and follow it east for 6.3 miles. Turn left onto Mills Gap Road. Go 0.3 miles and then turn right onto Bearwallow Road. Go 2.7 miles and make a left onto Clear Creek Road. You will go only 0.2 miles and then turn right onto Bearwallow Mountain Road. It is a five-mile winding drive up the mountain. You will go through the Grand Highlands estates. The trailhead and parking are at the road crest where the pavement changes to gravel. Limited parking spaces are available on the shoulder of the road. Please do not block the gate or the road.

You can also approach from the other side of the mountain, driving up Bearwallow Mountain Road from the little town of Gerton, North Carolina. Please note that the road is gravel for the last several miles up the mountain, so the way may be steep and bumpy.

« THE TRAIL—KEY FEATURES

0.0–0.5 MILES—A rusted locked gate marks the entrance to the property. The trail begins at the kiosk/sign on your right after you go around the gate. You will begin a gradual but steady climb through a series of switchbacks on the west side of the mountain. Take time to notice the wildflowers and ferns in spring and summer. When the leaves are down in fall and winter, stunning views are revealed.

0.5–0.7 MILES—The trail makes a sharp switchback and levels out as it curves around to the northern side of the mountain. You are treated to more vistas, changing vegetation, and interesting rocky outcroppings. You will climb several sets of rock stairs.

0.8–1.0 MILES—The trail emerges onto Bearwallow Mountain's meadow. Continue walking further up toward the fire tower and you will get even better views! Don't be surprised if you see cattle grazing on the meadow during the summer months.

You can reverse back down the trail to the parking area, or you may wish to return by the gravel service road, making a loop.

« Black Balsam Knob

The hike to Black Balsam Knob is a jewel in the crown of southern Appalachian balds. This very popular hike is easily accessible from the Blue Ridge Parkway (near milepost 420), and it's just a short half-mile climb to reach the summit. At 6,207 feet, Black Balsam Knob is the highest of all southern Appalachian balds. Much of the climb is in the open, so you'll have numerous opportunities to marvel at the ever-changing views as you make your way higher and higher. Face any direction and the landscape opens before you. To the east, you'll see the dome of Looking Glass Rock changing colors in the light. You'll also see the ribbon of the

Parkway winding its way through the mountain ridges. To the northeast, you'll see Mount Pisgah far off in the distance. To the north, follow the open ridgeline and you'll see the glowing white quartz that is Shining Rock. Face west and you'll see Sam Knob.

Note: A hike to the Sam Knob summit (see Sam Knob) offers an additional experience and can be done on the same day as your hike to Black Balsam Knob. Both trailheads are on Black Balsam Road.

HISTORICAL NOTE »

Several devastating fires have raged through this area, the most recent in 1942. The soil was severely damaged, slowing down the process of forest regrowth.

HIGHLIGHTS »

DISTANCE	»	Approximately one mile
TOTAL ASCENT	»	400 feet
ELEVATION START	»	5,800 feet (summit USGS benchmark 6,207 feet)
DIFFICULTY	»	Moderate
HIKING TIME	»	2 hours
USGS QUAD	»	Shining Rock
MAP	»	Pisgah Ranger District
MANAGED BY	»	U.S. Forest Service– Pisgah National Forest
FACILITIES AND FEES	»	No fees; no restrooms, no drinking water

Note: There are numerous opportunities to extend this hike. For example, you can easily go on to Tennet Mountain and Shining Rock or to Graveyard Fields. To consider different options, you may wish to view the Pisgah Ranger District trail map, National Geographic #780.

Black Balsam Knob

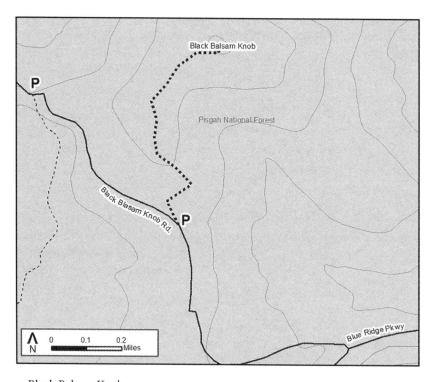

Black Balsam Knob

GETTING THERE »

The trailhead is located on Black Balsam Road (U.S. Forest Service #816) off the Blue Ridge Parkway at milepost 420.2. Drive down this paved road 0.8 miles and you'll see a small roadside parking area on the right. You will park there. This is the gap where the Art Loeb Trail and the Mountains to Sea Trail cross. The hike to Black Balsam Knob is actually a section of the Art Loeb Trail.

You can also park in the parking lot at the end of F.S. #816 and hike the Art Loeb Spur Trail to the Art Loeb Trail leading to Black Balsam.

THE TRAIL—KEY FEATURES »

0.0–0.2 MILES—The trailhead (a section of the Art Loeb Trail) opens to the right of the roadside parking and quickly enters a spruce-fir forest ecosystem, where cooler air, deep shadows, and the scent of evergreen envelope you.

0.2 MILES—You begin a gradual climb, and the trail breaks out of the forest into a rocky open meadow.

0.2–0.4 MILES—The trail begins an open climb to a smaller rocky summit where stunning views begin to unfold in all directions. The junction of the Art Loeb Spur Trail is to your left. Continue straight and you will see the trail as it climbs to the Black Balsam summit.

0.4–0.8 MILES—There is a kind of saddle after the first rocky outcropping, so there a slight descent before you make the final climb to the summit. You will want to explore a little, for the grassy meadow is quite large. There is a marker commemorating Art Loeb as well as a USGS benchmark—Silvermine 6,207 feet.

For the return, reverse your way back to the parking area.

« Craggy Knob at Craggy Gardens

The short hike on the Craggy Gardens Trail to the mixed grassy-and-heath summit of Craggy Knob (5,526 feet) is a perfect addition to a day exploring the Craggy Gardens section of the Blue Ridge Parkway, a section that is only 24 miles from Asheville, North Carolina. You can include this hike with a picnic at the Craggy Gardens Picnic Area, a stop at the Visitor Center, and another hike to the rocky summit of Craggy Pinnacle (5,892 feet). All are found between mileposts 367.6 and 364. At these high elevations, the views are spectacular, and there is great variety of terrain and plant life.

At Craggy Gardens you'll experience the mysterious, gnarled rhododendron tunnels that burst into bloom with a profusion of pinks and purples each June. The mixed grassy and heath summit is dominated by rhododendron and tasty blueberries in the fall, but you'll also see a variety of wildflowers such as violets, may apple, and the bright golden orange of Turk's-cap lilies.

« HIGHLIGHTS

FROM THE VISITOR CENTER

DISTANCE »	0.8 miles round-trip
TOTAL ASCENT »	207 feet
ELEVATION START »	5,424 feet
DIFFICULTY »	Easy
HIKING TIME »	30 minutes
USGS QUAD »	Craggy Pinnacle
MANAGED BY »	National Park Service–Blue Ridge Parkway
FACILITIES AND FEES »	Restrooms available, water available; no fees

Note: For additional hikes you can take portions of the Mountains-to-Sea Trail to the Snowball Mountain Trail or the Douglas Falls Trail.

FROM THE PICNIC AREA

DISTANCE	»	1.2 miles round-trip
TOTAL ASCENT	»	410 feet
ELEVATION START	»	5,221 feet
DIFFICULTY	»	Easy/Moderate
HIKING TIME	»	1 hour
USGS QUAD	»	Craggy Pinnacle
TRAIL MAP	»	National Park Service, Blue Ridge Parkway
MANAGED BY	»	National Park Service
FACILITIES AND FEES	»	Restrooms available, water available; no fees

Note: For additional hikes you can take portions of the Mountains-to-Sea Trail to the Snowball Mountain Trail or the Douglas Falls Trail

GETTING THERE »

The Craggy Gardens area is located on a section of the Blue Ridge Parkway between Asheville, North Carolina, and Little Switzerland, North Carolina, between milepost 367.6 (road to the picnic area) and 364.5 (Visitor Center) and then 364 (parking for Craggy Pinnacle Trail).

THE TRAIL—KEY FEATURES »

FROM THE VISITOR CENTER

0.0–0.2 MILES—Begin the hike at a trailhead located at the south end of the Visitor Center parking lot. Continue along this self-guided trail for a gentle climb through a mixed hardwood forest. Bypass the Douglas Falls Trail, which branches off to the right at an intersection just beyond the start of the hike.

Craggy Gardens

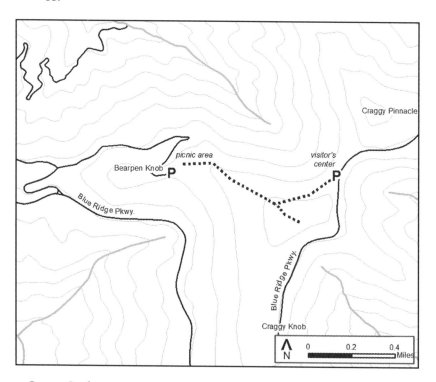

Craggy Gardens

0.2–0.4 MILES—The trail leaves the forest and arrives at a covered shelter. Take a left at the shelter and follow the trail, which winds its way up through an open grassy heath community. Take time to explore the side paths that cross the meadow. The main trail ends at a 5,631-foot stone lookout where you will have great views of the town of Montreat and the Black Mountain range.

FROM THE PICNIC AREA

0.0–0.4 MILES—Begin the hike at a trailhead located at the far end of the picnic-area parking lot. Follow the trail for a moderate ascent through a mixed hardwood forest. This section of the trail is slightly rocky and relatively steep, incurring an elevation gain of about 400 feet.

0.4–0.6 MILES—The trail leaves the forest and arrives at a historic wooden trail shelter. You may want to sit a moment to catch your breath. Look to your right, and you will see a side trail leading up over the grassy summit. Make sure you take time to explore this trail, for expansive vistas will now open before you. The trail crosses the summit and ends at a 5,631-foot stone lookout, where you have great views of the town of Montreat and the Black Mountain Range.

Max Patch Mountain »

For me, Max Patch is one of the crown jewels of the Appalachian balds. With a round-trip of 1.4 miles and an elevation gain of only 265 feet, the hike is perfect for families with young children out for a summer picnic, a day of kite flying, or a night of star gazing. Although the summit is lower in elevation than that of many other balds (4,629 feet), you'll feel you're on top of the world when you arrive at the huge open meadow there. Face any direction and you'll see breathtaking views—mountain ranges rippling one after another in the distance, and to the west Mount Sterling and Mount Cammerer. Stroll around or lie down in the soft grasses and experience the world at ground level; you'll see a stunning display of wildflowers in the spring, summer, or fall. On clear nights, Max Patch becomes what some have called "nature's planetarium." You'll feel you are where the earth meets the sky, making for a spectacular stargazing experience away from urban lights.

Max Patch Summit

View from Max Patch Summit

Flame Azalea

Catawba Rhododendron

Turk's Cap Lily

Bee Balm

Azalea Display on Gregory Bald

Azalea Display on Gregory Bald. Courtesy of Nicholas Lenze

Mountain Laurel

Gray's Lily on Jane Bald. Courtesy of Nicholas Lenze

Deer on Gregory Bald. Courtesy of Nicholas Lenze

Gregory Bald

Max Patch

View from Hemphill Bald

Fall is on the way at Purchase Knob

Fall View from the Trail to Hemphill Bald

View from the summit of Hemphill Bald

Mother and Foal—Trail to Mt. Rogers

View on the Trail to Mt. Rogers

View on the Trail to Little Hump Mountain

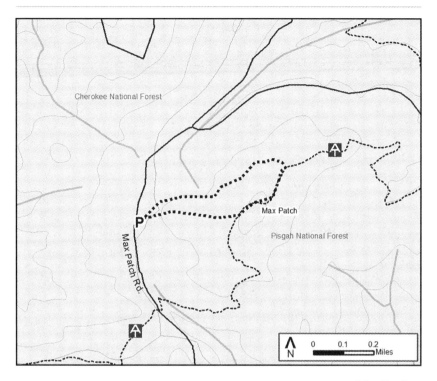

Max Patch

HISTORICAL NOTES »

Max Patch has had a long pattern of human use or "disturbance," as ecologists would say. Historical records tell us early settlers brought their livestock up to graze on the lush grassy summit during the summer months. It is also said that the meadow was used as a landing strip in the 1920s and that, for a small fee, visitors were taken on short flights to see the view from above (Hiking the Carolinas). It's astounding that Max Patch still exists today for us to enjoy, for in the 1980s a developer wanted to build a resort there. Fortunately, Arch Nichols, a long-time member of the Carolina Mountain Club and a supporter of the Appalachian Trail effort, was instrumental in saving the bald. It was incorporated into national forest land, and today the U.S. Forest Service, in collaboration with the Appalachian Trail Conservancy, actively maintains the bald. A very popular section of the AT crosses the summit. As a matter of fact, most of the trail described here is a part of this segment of the AT (Adkins and ATC, 8).

« HIGHLIGHTS

DISTANCE	»	1.4-mile loop to summit, 2.4-mile loop around base
ASCENT	»	265 feet
ELEVATION START	»	4,364 feet
DIFFICULTY	»	Moderate easy
HIKING TIME	»	1 hours
USGS QUAD	»	Lemon Gap
MANAGED BY	»	Pisgah National Forest and Appalachian Trail Conservancy
FACILITIES AND FEES	»	No fees, no restrooms, no drinking water

Note: The signs to the trailhead are not well marked.

« GETTING THERE

From Asheville: Take I-40 West to Exit 7 (Harmon's Den). Take a right on Cold Springs Road. The road almost immediately becomes gravel. Continue 6.2 miles as the road makes a steady continual climb to SR-1182 (Max Patch Road). Beware—there is no trail sign/road sign indicating Max Patch. Turn left and drive 1.5 miles to the Max Patch parking area on the right.

« THE TRAIL—KEY FEATURES

0.0 MILE—The trailhead for the 1.4-mile loop is located at the end of the parking lot. There are three unmarked trails at this junction, so it may be confusing. The leftmost trail is the beginning of the 1.4-mile loop. The middle trail is the return segment of this loop. If you wish to go directly up to the summit, bypassing the majority of the loop, you may take this trail. The third trail on the far right is the beginning of a 2.4-mile loop that circles the mountain, allowing for a different perspective.

0.0–0.40 MILES—Take the trail to the left and almost immediately enter a mixed hardwood forest scattered with clusters of blackberry and blueberry bushes. There is a gentle climb through this section.

0.40–0.70 MILES—The trail breaks out of the forest onto the bald. You are greeted by the open sky and the smell of grasses and wildflowers. In several hundred feet you will reach a trail junction. Take a right onto the AT and follow the white-painted posts up to the summit. This section is only slightly steeper.

0.70 MILES—Take time to explore the summit, take photos, have a picnic, fly a kite, and soak in the incredible views. The 350-acre grassy summit offers plenty of room to immerse yourself in the beauty of the bald. Or you may want to strike up a conversation with other hikers, including intrepid adventurers trekking this section of the AT.

0.70–1.4 MILES—Take the trail that leads back down to the parking lot to complete the loop. You are able to see the parking lot from the top of the bald.

Purchase Knob–Great Smoky Mountains National Park and Hemphill Bald »

This lovely hike offers you the opportunity to experience two high-elevation grassy balds within a single hike. There are also two options—the shorter four-mile loop takes you by the historic Ferguson Cabin, the highest-elevation log cabin in the Smokies, and then up to the Appalachian Highlands Science Learning Center at Purchase Knob (National Park Service, signage). At an altitude of almost 5,000 feet, the world opens before you with a stunning view of Purchase Knob as well as the etched outlines of Mount Pisgah and Cold Mountain in the distance. This hike has much to offer, and the changing seasons make each visit unique. In the fall, leaves create a colorful blanket of oranges, reds, yellows, and gold draped over the extensive hardwood forest below. The grasses on the summit are sprinkled with wildflowers spring through fall, bringing varied palettes of color with each season.

Purchase Knob. Courtesy of Nicholas Lenze

Hemphill Bald

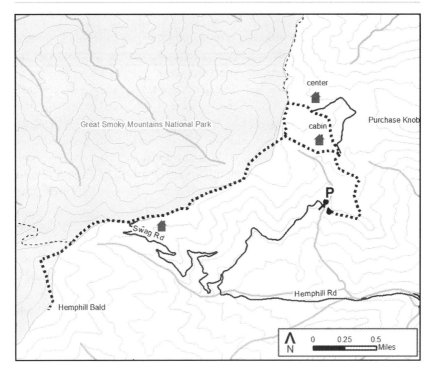

Purchase Knob–Hemphill Bald

The second option extends the hike to a captivating 8.24-mile round-trip hike to Hemphill Bald, returning via the Learning Center at Purchase Knob. There are several points of interest along the hike that serve to broaden the experience, including the two grassy bald areas, the Appalachian Highlands Science Learning Center, Ferguson Cabin, the Swag Country Inn, and Cataloochee Ranch. Underlying these features is an unwavering sense of the beauty of the natural world. Located in Great Smoky Mountains National Park and spanning a large part of the Cataloochee ridgeline, the hike naturally offers sweeping views without the price of a continuous steep ascent. Along the entire route, the trail is well maintained and "easy on the feet."

HISTORICAL NOTES »

An interesting aspect of this hike arises from the history of each of its two featured grassy bald areas. The grassy knoll upon which the Science Learning Center sits was part of a 535-acre donation to Great Smoky

Mountains Park by Kathryn McNeil and Voit Gilmore in 2000. The property had served as their summer retreat since 1964 and included a home, tennis courts, hiking trails, meadows, and more (Lix, 38–45). McNeil and Gilmore loved the property too much to see it developed. With that in mind, the family contacted Park officials in the 1990s to see if they would be interested in receiving the property, since it was contiguous with the Park boundary. McNeil explained that "it's time to pass it into other hands who would leave its meadows, forests, and hundred mile views just as they were" (Lix, 38–45). This is the twist or irony to the name Purchase Knob—it is the largest gift of property from a private donor in the history of the Park (Lix, 38–45). Now we all can benefit from this amazing legacy!

According to information provided by the National Park Service, included in their donation were the family summer home, the historic Ferguson Cabin, and Purchase Knob. Congress converted the summer home into the Appalachian Highlands Science Learning Center in 2001 to support research in the National Park and as a means for sharing this research with the public. Ferguson Cabin, named after John Ferguson, who built the log cabin in 1874 as a dwelling place for his family, remains preserved as a historic landmark and is open to visitors. This huge inclusive donation to the National Park attracts thousands of visitors each year, among them students, families, and scientists (National Park Service, "About Purchase Knob"). Hemphill Bald, the second grassy bald area and the final destination for this hike, is part of another public gift. In 1993, Tom Alexander Jr., a descendent of the original owners of Cataloochee Ranch, generously placed 220 acres of land into a conservation easement with the Southern Appalachian Highlands Conservancy. This land included Hemphill Bald and the adjacent Thunderbolt Knob (SAHC, "Focus Areas"). According to the Conservancy, "Cataloochee Ranch serves as critical link to Great Smoky Mountains National Park; the ranch provides a valuable refuge for wildlife on the boundary of the Park, including a number of threatened migratory song birds. Because of conservation easements on the property, Cataloochee Ranch will continue to be enjoyed by generations to come" (SAHC, "Focus Areas").

Hemphill Bald, although still privately owned, is a wonderful example of a personal commitment to the protection and conservation of these special places. The 300-acre Cataloochee Ranch, which offers lodging, horseback riding, hiking, and more, has been family owned and managed by three generations (SAHC, "Focus Areas").

From Hemphill Bald, there are views down into the ranch and extending to the horizon, capturing several notables: Mount Pisgah, Cold Mountain, Mount Mitchell, Purchase Knob, and Jonathan Valley. Together, the hike along the Cataloochee ridgeline and its culmination at the magnificent grassy façade of Hemphill Bald create an experience of natural beauty that is well worth the visit.

HIGHLIGHTS »

DISTANCE »	4-mile loop or 8.24-mile loop
ASCENT »	1,362 feet
ELEVATION START »	4,188 feet
DIFFICULTY »	Moderate (4-mile loop); Strenuous— the entire hike
HIKING TIME »	2.5 or 5.5 hours
USGS QUAD »	Dellwood
MANAGED BY »	National Park Service
FACILITIES AND FEES »	No fees; Restrooms at Science Learning Center may or may not be open.

Note: The signs to the trailhead are not well marked.

GETTING THERE »

From Asheville, take I-40 West to exit 20. Follow U.S. Highway 276 east toward Maggie Valley. In 3.0 miles turn right on Grindstone Road. Continue on Grindstone Road for one mile, then turn right onto Hemphill Road. Continue about 4.0 miles until you reach a gate and sign marking the entrance to Great Smoky Mountains National Park and Purchase Knob. You will park at the small gravel pullout on your left just before the gate. (The gate closes at dusk, so even if it is open, you will likely want to park outside the gate.) Be sure not to block the road to the Learning Center.

1.0–1.15 MILES—Walk past the gate and along a scenic gravel road. This road makes a gentle climb through a hardwood forest. Arrive at the Ferguson Cabin Trial sign on the left. The Science Learning Center can be seen on the grassy knoll in the distance.

1.15–1.52 MILES—Follow the Ferguson Cabin Trail down to the cabin. Take a few minutes to explore the historic log home. Continue on the Ferguson Cabin Trail, which picks up in the forest beyond the cabin, and follow the signs to the Cataloochee Divide Trail.

1.52 MILES—Arrive at the Cataloochee Divide Trail junction. You now have two options—a 4-mile round-trip loop to the Science Learning Center and back to the gate or a longer hike (8.2 miles) to Hemphill Bald and back down past the Learning Center.

For the shorter loop hike, take a right and continue on the Cataloochee Divide Trail, maintaining a slight ascent. After you have gone about 0.4 miles, you will come upon a trail sign on the left side and a "no horses" sign directly across on the right. *There is no clear indication, but you must take a right onto the trail marked by the "no horses" sign.* You will continue on this trail for about 0.3 miles until you reach the Science Learning Center. Take time to explore the Science Learning Center and enjoy the outstanding views. Then complete the loop by continuing on the trail, which picks up below the Science Learning Center and descends through the grassy meadow to the gravel road below.

To continue to the Swag (1 mile) and Hemphill Bald (1.8 miles), take a left at this junction. You are on the Cataloochee Divide Trail as it begins a moderate climb through a hardwood forest. Follow the signs to Double

Gap. Since you are on the ridgeline at 5,000 feet, you'll be treated to views to the left and right depending on the time of year.

1.52—2.56 MILES—You'll note the Swag (Country Inn) property that opens to the left, offering stunning mountains vistas with a view of Hemphill Bald off to the right. This is private property, so please be respectful when walking out to enjoy the views. Re-enter the trail and continue.

2.56–3.32 MILES—Continue on the Cataloochee Divide Trail to Double Gap.

3.32–4.12 MILES—Arrive at Double Gap, which sits at 5,080 feet. You will come upon a marked trail junction at the base of an open grassy mountainside. Continue straight at this junction and follow the trail that runs along the outside of the fence. You will quickly re-enter a shaded forest and begin a steep ascent up to the top of Hemphill Bald.

4.12 MILES—Exit the forest and go through the gated fence on the left that leads out onto the 5,550-foot Hemphill Bald. The area on this side of the gate is part of the Cataloochee Ranch, so take care to show respect for the property. Let the beauty of the open bald and its accompanying views envelope you; they are truly spectacular. There is a stone picnic table to the right with a map that will help you identify all of the surrounding mountains. The bald area is quite extensive, and you can walk through the grass to the left to explore the adjacent pinnacle, Thunderbolt Knob, before heading back.

On the return trip, you may retrace your path back down the Cataloochee Divide Trail, the Ferguson Cabin Trail, and the gravel road back to the gate.

Alternatively, after reaching the junction for the Ferguson Cabin Trail, you may continue straight on the Divide Trail. After about 0.4

miles, you will come upon a trail sign on the left side and a "no horses" sign directly across on the right. *There is no clear indication, but you must take a right onto the trail marked by the "no horses" sign.* You will continue on this trail for about 0.3 miles until you reach the Science Learning Center. Look around the Science Learning Center and admire the outstanding views. Then continue on the trail, which picks up below the Science Learning Center and descends through the grassy meadow to the gravel road below. Walk down the gravel road to the gate and your car.

« Sam Knob

Although Sam Knob is not an open grassy summit, it is a fine example of a heath bald ecosystem, with blueberries galore (in late August), grasses, rocky outcroppings, and extensive panoramic views. It is a fine hike to do in conjunction with the Black Balsam Knob hike if time permits, since both trailheads are located on Black Balsam Road. The Sam Knob hike is also an excellent hike for a hot summer day. Since you start at one of the highest-altitude trailheads in the area, nearly 6,000 feet, the temperatures rarely climb above the mid-70s to low 80s.

The hike itself is a delight, for it takes you through a meadow often filled with wildflowers, butterflies, and birds. You then begin a series of

Sam Knob

Sam Knob

switchbacks making their ascent to the summit through a fern-filled forest
understory, tunnels of mountain laurel. and Catawba rhododendron; then
the trail winds its way up rocky outcroppings near the summit. You will
get spectacular views of the meadow below, Black Balsam Knob and the
Devil's Courthouse.

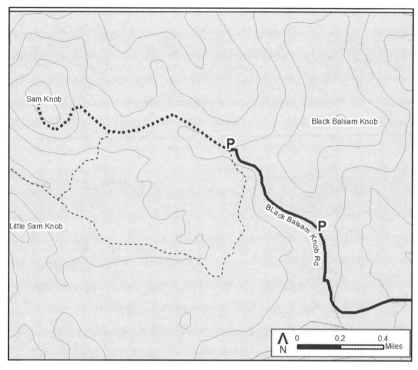

Sam Knob

HIGHLIGHTS »

DISTANCE » **2.64 miles round-trip**

ASCENT » **570 feet**

ELEVATION START » **5,835 feet (the trail descends to a
grassy meadow before makes its
ascent to the 6,050 foot summit)**

DIFFICULTY » **Moderate**

HIKING TIME » **2 hours**

USGS QUAD	»	Sam Knob
MANAGED BY	»	Pisgah National Forest
FACILITIES AND FEES	»	No fees; restrooms available, no water

« GETTING THERE

The road to the Sam Knob parking lot is located between mile markers 420 and 421 on the Blue Ridge Parkway. From Asheville, take the Blue Ridge Parkway south for about 30 miles. Turn right on FR 816 (Black Balsam Road) just past milepost 420. Follow this road about one mile to the end at the parking area.

« THE TRAIL—KEY FEATURES

0.0–0.5 MILES—Begin the hike on a trail located directly to the right of the outhouse, marked only by a post that says "keep right at junctions." The trail enters brushy vegetation and then makes a gentle descent along wooden boardwalks into a picturesque grassy meadow.

0.5–0.62 MILES—After crossing the meadow, take a right at a trail junction toward Sam Knob Summit. The trail navigates a moderate ascent with a series of switchbacks through a dense heath ecosystem. Shortly, you will emerge and begin to see views at a surprisingly high vantage point.

0.62–1.32 MILES—Continue along the rocky trail, which wraps its way around the southeast side of the mountain. Along this entire stretch you will be able to gaze down on the soft buttery meadow, bisected smoothly by the trail, and across to the massive grass sheath of Black Balsam Knob.

1.32 MILES—Arrive at the summit of Sam Knob and absorb the ever-so-invigorating "on-top-of-the-world" feeling. Explore the summit for that perfect spot for picnic and numerous views. From this 6,050-foot vantage point, you will be able to see Fork Mountain, Fork Ridge, and Devil's Courthouse as part of the vast mountain landscape.

Note: Because there are considerable rocky outcroppings, pay special attention where you walk or sit. Snakes may be utilizing the rocks to bask in the sun.

Cherohala Skyway Area

Bob Stratton Bald. Courtesy of Nicholas Lenze

The Cherohala Skyway is aptly named, for it snakes its way along high mountain elevations between the small towns of Robbinsville, North Carolina, and Tellico Plains, Tennessee. Designated a National Scenic Byway, the 43-mile-long Skyway offers superb mountain views along its many overlooks. It passes through both the Cherokee and Nantahala National Forests—hence the name *Chero-hala* (Town of Tellico Plains, "Guide to Tellico Plains—Cherohala Skyway").

« Bob Stratton Bald

This trail is the longest of four bald hikes located along the Cherohala Skyway. Stratton Bald is located in the Joyce Kilmer-Slickrock Wilderness, a seventeen-thousand acre tract bordering North Carolina and Tennessee. The Wilderness was created by Congress in 1975 and named in honor of the poet and journalist Joyce Kilmer, who was killed in action in World War I. He is famous for his beautiful poem "Trees." It is fitting, then, that the Wilderness, as well the Joyce Kilmer Memorial Forest, is a prime example of a cove hardwood forest, where some trees have a 20-foot circumference and are possibly 400 years old (U.S. Forest Service, "Joyce Kilmer Memorial Forest").

The 6.4-mile round-trip hike to Bob Stratton Bald offers a welcome serenity. You can feel the wonder articulated in Kilmer's poem "Trees." Towering hardwoods and conifers surround you. It is truly a peaceful trail. As you ascend the 5,341-foot bald, the air thins, and the giant trees transition into rhododendron and mountain laurel. Upon reaching the grassy bald summit of the mountain, you'll feel a sense of wonder consistent with the rest of the hike. As you walk out into the meadow, you will have extraordinary views of the Unicoi Mountains and valley below.

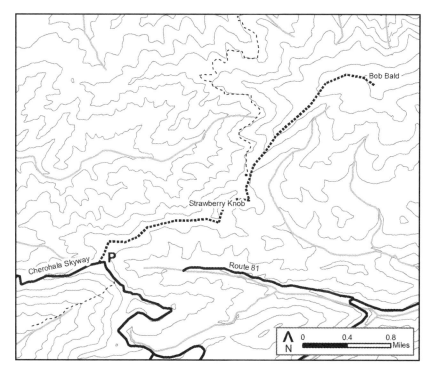

Bob Stratton Bald

« HISTORICAL NOTE

As with all of the balds, the area is steeped in a rich history. As you stand on the summit, it's also worth taking a moment to ponder and absorb the past. The bald and the surrounding area were home to several generations of Strattons. In a colorful passage John Preston Arthur in his *History of Western North Carolina (1730–1913)* wrote, "John and Robert Stratton came from Monroe county, Tenn., in the thirties and settled on the Unaka mountains between the head of the Sassafras ridge and Santeetla creek. John lived on the John Stratton Bald ten years and caught 19 panthers on the Laurel Top, making 'bacon' of their hams and shoulders. He came with nothing but his rifle, blanket, skillet and ammunition, but made enough herding cattle and selling deer and bear hams and hides, etc., to buy a fine farm in Monroe county, Tenn." (212). The beauty and serenity of the hike through this wilderness area, the views from the summit, and the opportunity to ponder generations from long ago make this hike a must-do.

« HIGHLIGHTS

DISTANCE	»	6.4 miles
TOTAL ASCENT	»	845 feet
ELEVATION START	»	4,496 feet
DIFFICULTY	»	Strenuous
HIKING TIME	»	4.5 hours
USGS QUAD	»	Big Junction
MANAGED BY	»	U.S. Forest Service– North Carolina Forests
FACILITIES AND FEES	»	No fees

Note: There is some discrepancy in names. The USGS topo map shows this as Bob Bald, with another point marked Stratton Bald. There are several locations named for one or more of the Strattons from several generations. Other hiking descriptions describe this bald as Stratton Bald or Bob Stratton Bald.

Coming from Robbinsville, follow the Cherohala Skyway to the Unicoi Crest Parking Area. You can park here and then walk up the highway several hundred feet until you reach the North Carolina–Tennessee state line, or you may park your car on the side of the road at the state line. The hike begins on the Benton MacKaye Trail. The trailhead is located right before you reach the state line on the right side of the road; it begins as a gated forest service road.

Since this is a designated "wilderness" area, trails are only minimally maintained. No trail blazes are allowed, and only small wooden signs are located at trail junctures. Routes can be confusing.

THE TRAIL—KEY FEATURES »

0.0 MILES—You will start the hike on the Benton MacKaye Trail. It begins as an old forest service road branching off the Cherohala Skyway. Walk around the gated entrance of the forest service road; the gate is marked by a white diamond to indicate that it is part the Benton MacKaye Trail.

0.0–1.91 MILES—You will follow the Benton MacKaye Trail along the old forest service road and quickly enter a mixed hardwood-evergreen forest. The trail travels along a ridgeline that separates two protected areas, each known for its unique flora and untouched natural beauty: the Citico Creek Wilderness to the left and the Joyce Kilmer–Slickrock Wilderness to the right. You will encounter a relatively gentle climb and tranquil shade for the majority of this section.

1.91 MILES—You will come upon a minimally marked trail junction. There is no sign for Stratton Bald. Take the *unmarked* trail that veers to right that has a "Pack, Sack and Draft Animals Prohibited" sign (do *not* take the trail to the left that has a sign for #95 Fodderstack Trail and the Citico Creek Wilderness).

1.92–2.88 MILES—You will begin a very steep ascent toward Stratton Bald. Continue along this trail, which eventually levels out onto a beautiful ridgeline. The ridgeline is sprinkled with softly colored rhododendron and mountain laurel that perfectly enhance the foreground of open sky that extends beyond.

2.88 MILES—You will come upon another minimally marked trail junction. Again, there is no sign for Stratton Bald. Continue straight on the trail that you have been on, which is indicated as #54 on the wooden post. There is a trail that is indicated by a wooden post as #59a, branching off to the left—*do not take it.*

2.88–3.2 MILES—Continue along the high-elevation ridgeline, maintaining a gentle climb. At 3.2 miles and 5,341 feet, you will arrive at the grassy summit of Stratton Bald on the right. The grassy area opens to the southwest, with views across the valley into the rippling Unicoi Mountains of North Carolina. A section of the Cherohala Skyway can be seen as it weaves around the rim of a mountain in the distance. The bald area is small enough to walk around and explore; it is interspersed with a diverse collection of young trees and shrubbery, along with a buzzing community of life.

« Hooper Bald

Hooper Bald is one of four balds featured in this guide having trailheads located along the Cherohala Skyway. The hike to Hooper Bald is an easy one and well worth the adventure. With only a half-mile of hiking required to reach this captivating grassy bald, this is a popular leg-stretcher for travelers of the Cherohala Skyway. Although Hooper Bald is located only a mile down the highway from Huckleberry Knob, it offers a completely distinctive experience, pleasingly unique. The bald area, which is perched at 5,429 feet, is blanketed in creamy grass continuously rolling in the wind. Depending on the time of year, you may see an abundance of flame azaleas, mountain laurel, or Turk's cap lilies. Some of the vistas from Hooper are obscured by trees, but you will be treated to a great view of the grassy cap of its neighbor, Huckleberry Knob, to the north.

Hooper Bald

HISTORICAL NOTES »

How did Hooper Bald get its name? One family history states that Hooper Bald was named for Enos Hooper, who moved, with his wife, Margaret Harbison Hooper, to Graham County, North Carolina, from Monroe County, Tennessee, in 1840. He was the area's first doctor and was said to have acquired several thousand acres of land that had opened up to homesteaders after the forced removal of the Cherokee to Oklahoma by the federal government. Enos began to graze cattle on the high mountain meadows, including Hooper Bald. The Hoopers even raised a special breed of pony, called the Hooper pony, to herd cattle (McClung, "Hooper Bald").

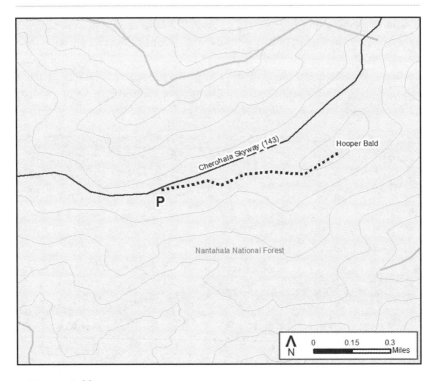

Hooper Bald

In addition to the story about how Hooper Bald got its name, there are other tidbits to ponder as you walk to the meadow. In 1908, George Moore, an agent for the Whiting Manufacturing Company (which then owned the land), decided to create a hunting preserve on Hooper Bald for wealthy clients, even building a lodge. Wild boar, buffalo, elk, mule deer, black bear, and Russian brown bear were imported for the preserve, and a ten-room hunting lodge was built below the bald. Most of the exotic animals eventually disappeared. However, the wild boar dug under the fences, reproduced, and thrived in the wild (McClung, "Hooper Bald").

Finally, there is possible evidence of much earlier European exploration. There is an inscription in Spanish on a large rock on Hooper Bald that is dated September 15, 1615. It reads *predarmscasada*. It's been there as long as anyone can remember, but no one knows if the inscription is authentic. The date doesn't match the time periods that Hernando de Soto or Juan Pardo were in the area. However, some believe that expedition members may have deserted and made these high mountains their home. There is also speculation about the meaning of the inscription. One idea is that the word combination indicates that someone was claiming the property as his own. Others have focused on the word *casada,* which means "married," and speculated that a couple got married on a spectacular open summit many years ago and inscribed the event on the rock.

Hooper Bald Lodge—1937. From the Albert "Dutch" Roth Digital Photograph Collection, courtesy of Charles Roth and the Great Smoky Mountains Regional Project, University of Tennessee Libraries

HIGHLIGHTS »

DISTANCE	»	1.0 miles round-trip
ASCENT	»	139 feet
ELEVATION START	»	5,290 feet
DIFFICULTY	»	Easy
HIKING TIME	»	50 minutes
USGS QUAD	»	Santeetlah Creek
MANAGED BY	»	U.S. Forest Service
FACILITIES AND FEES	»	Restrooms, but no drinking water; no fees

Huckleberry Knob

« GETTING THERE

The trailhead is located on the Cherohala Skyway. You will park in the Hooper Bald parking lot near mile marker #10. There is a large sign marking the trailhead and featuring details of the hike.

Note: The mile marker numbering begins with #1 at Robbinsville and ends with #43 at Tellico Plains.

« THE TRAIL—KEY FEATURES

0.0–0.5 MILES—The entire hike follows a well-marked, well-maintained gravel trail. You will begin the hike by walking up a flight of stairs on the right side of the parking lot. From here, the trail continues through a shaded hardwood forest. Much of the surrounding forest is carpeted in a soft grass, providing evidence of the once larger borders of the bald. At times there is a very gentle climb.

0.5 MILES—You will ascend one more flight of stairs, and Hooper Bald will open up right before your eyes. Take a left to explore a garden of flame azaleas, evergreens, and mountain laurel that inhabit the meadow. Take a right to continue for about a quarter of a mile out onto the 5,429-foot summit of Hooper Bald, where there is a great view of Huckleberry Knob to the north.

Reverse your way back down the trail to the parking lot.

« Huckleberry Knob

Huckleberry Knob is the third of four balds featured in this guide with trailheads are located along the Cherohala Skyway. At 5,560 feet, it is the highest point in the Cheoah Ranger District, and the summit offers spectacular panoramic views of the Unicoi Mountains. However, what makes it really special is that it offers two "bald experiences" in single 2.5-mile round-trip hike. The trail follows an old road bed and, at less than one-half mile, you step out into a picturesque meadow, rounded and soft with stunning views. This is Oak Knob. Although the knob is beautiful any time, in midsummer a sea of buttercups creates a canvas of soft yellows—nature's own impressionistic painting! Look to the left and you will see Huckleberry Knob and the trail leading to the summit. Once you reach the crest, the view back down to Oak Knob is striking.

In addition to the wonderful floral communities that grace these two grassy ecosystems, you are likely to see some key species of the birds that thrive in the bald habitat, including the bobwhite quail, the rufous-sided towhee, and the indigo bunting.

Huckleberry Knob

HISTORICAL NOTE »

There is an interesting slice of history associated with Huckleberry, as you'll see on the signage at the kiosk by the trailhead. The sign tells the

story of two men, Andy Sherman and Paul O'Neil, who left the Tellico
Creek logging camp on December 11, 1899, in an effort to reach Robbinsville by Christmas. Because of the harsh weather conditions, they
never arrived. Their bodies were found by a deer hunter nine months later
on Huckleberry Knob, along with several jugs of whiskey. A large white
cross currently marks Sherman's grave on Huckleberry. Paul O'Neil's
body was given to a medical exhibit. In sharp contrast to the stunning
and magical views, this simple white cross reminds visitors of the reality
of nature's power at these high elevations.

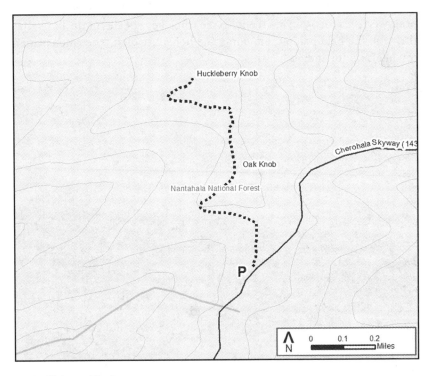

Huckleberry Knob

« HIGHLIGHTS

DISTANCE	»	1.92 miles round-trip
ASCENT	»	260 feet
ELEVATION START	»	5,300 feet

DIFFICULTY	»	Moderately easy
HIKING TIME	»	1.5 hours
USGS QUAD	»	Santeetlah Creek
MANAGED BY	»	U.S. Forest Service–Nantahala National Forest
FACILITIES AND FEES	»	No fees; no restrooms, no drinking water

GETTING THERE »

The trailhead is located on the Cherohala Skyway. You will park in the Huckleberry Bald parking lot near mile marker #9. There is a large sign marking the trailhead and featuring details of the hike. Mile marker numbering begins with #1 at Robbinsville and ends with #43 at Tellico Plains.

THE TRAIL—KEY FEATURES »

0.0–0.38 MILES—The Huckleberry Knob trailhead is marked by a large sign at the parking area. This first section of the trail is an old roadbed, wide and easy on the feet. Follow the trail through a mixed hardwood forest—a gentle climb.

0.38 MILES—The forest opens out into Oak Knob, a beautiful grassy bald nestled on the 5,440-foot mountaintop that lies next to Huckleberry Knob. Look up to the left to see the grassy cap of Huckleberry Knob.

0.38–0.61 MILES—The trail traverses across Oak Knob. Take time to explore this picturesque meadow.

0.61–0.84 MILES—Re-enter the hardwood forest after you cross Oak Knob, and continue on the trail toward Huckleberry Knob. The trail slightly steepens during this section.

> 0.84 MILES—The trail bursts out onto the grassy bald. You immediately experience that sense of exhilaration created by the grassy expanse that is mounted at 5,560 feet within the Unicoi Mountain range. It's truly liberating.
>
> 0.84–0.96 MILES—For the best vistas, follow the trail up to the summit. Here, you will have long-range views of the Unicoi Mountains in every direction. You will also be able to see the grassy patches of Oak Knob and Hooper Bald to the south. Also, you will pass the stark white cross marking the grave of Andy Sherman, one of two loggers who died here during the winter of 1899.
>
> Reverse your way back down the trail to the parking area.

« Whigg Meadow

Whigg Meadow is the fourth of four grassy balds located along the Cherohala Skyway. The trail to the summit is actually a tiny section of the Benton MacKaye Trail, a 300-mile footpath that traverses the southern Appalachian backcountry from north Georgia to the northern edge of Great Smoky Mountains National Park. Hailed in the *New York Times* as "one of the most breathtaking spots on the Benton MacKaye," Whigg Meadow is a "flower-filled mountaintop grassland" whose beauty is well worth a visit (Dixon). When the trail suddenly emerges from the forest, you will see an arc of open meadow rising where the earth meets the sky. After a gentle climb to the summit, at 4,958 feet, you'll have the sensation of standing on top of a quiet, friendly giant, feeling as if you are above everything else, serenely surveying the world before your eyes.

« HISTORICAL NOTE

The origin of Whigg Meadow, as a grassy opening in the forest canopy, is unclear. There is some evidence that it was cleared or expanded by the Whigg and Hooper families. Like most other grassy balds, Whigg Meadow does have a history of grazing. There was also a cabin, explained as a small shepherd's cabin, on the property (U.S. Forest Service, signage).

Whigg Meadow

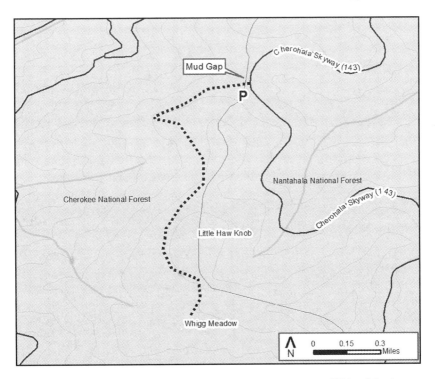

Whigg Meadow

It may have also served as a hunter's camp in the early 1900s (McClung, "About Hooper Bald and the Surrounding Areas"). Although the cabin is gone, some split-rail fences remain. Also, a spring and pond at the edge of the meadow are thought to be near the site of the cabin. It is currently being maintained as a grassy meadow by the U.S. Forest Service.

« HIGHLIGHTS

DISTANCE	»	3.0 miles round-trip
TOTAL ASCENT	»	478 feet
ELEVATION START	»	4,480 feet
DIFFICULTY	»	Moderately easy
HIKING TIME	»	2 hours
USGS QUAD	»	Big Junction, Tennessee
MANAGED BY	»	Cherokee National Forest
FACILITIES AND FEES	»	No fees; no restrooms, no drinking water

« GETTING THERE

The trailhead is located on the Cherohala Skyway. You will park in the Mud Gap parking lot near mile marker #3 on the North Carolina side. There is a large sign marking the trailhead and explaining the hike.

« THE TRAIL—KEY FEATURES

0.0–1.5 MILES—The hike to Whigg Meadow utilizes a section the Benton MacKaye Trail, an old four-wheel-drive road. You will begin the hike at the Mud Gap Trailhead, which is located at the end of the parking lot. The trail travels south along the mountainside through a lush hardwood forest. There are occasional views into the valley when you look off the ridge to the right. The trail is moderately steep and slightly rocky for the majority of the hike. As you near Whigg Meadow, blackberry bushes line the trail, making for a tasty reward in the late summer.

1.5 MILES—The trail meets with a forest service road, and the grassy Whigg Meadow pops out to the right. Embrace the sky as you walk up to the 4,958-foot summit, where you will find spectacular views of endless mountain ranges, sweeping valleys, and lakes shaped like blue jigsaw puzzle pieces. You can also walk around the edge of the bald, where you will find bushes loaded with ripe blueberries in late August and a small tucked-away pond.

Return down the trail to the Mud Gap parking area.

Great Smoky Mountains National Park

Andrews Bald, at 5,920 feet, is the highest bald summit in Great Smoky Mountains National Park. It is one of two natural grassy balds in the Park that are actively managed by the National Park Service.

« Andrews Bald

Offering superb high-elevation views, it has been a popular hiking destination for many years. The trailhead is located at the end of the bustling parking lot for Clingmans Dome. At 6,643 feet, the Dome is the highest peak in Great Smoky Mountains National Park. As a bonus to the hike, you may want to take the steep 0.5-mile walk to the peak's observation tower, which is a popular tourist stop because of its famous 360-degree panoramic views.

The hike to Andrews Bald provides a different experience than the busy Clingmans Dome observation tower does. Quickly abandoning the noise of people and cars, you enter a serene spruce-fir forest complemented by the scent of fresh evergreen and an occasional breeze. At several points along the trail, the forest opens up with outstanding views of Forney Ridge. At the summit, you realize why it's such a popular hike. From the southern edge, there are beautiful views of Fontana Lake to the southwest, the Great Smoky Mountains to the west, and the Nantahala Mountains to the south. Along with the grasses and wildflowers, wild azaleas and Catawba rhododendron sprinkle the meadow in the summer.

Since the summit is usually the focus, many hikers fail to mention the beauty of the hike itself as it descends through rocky outcroppings and spruce-fir forest before exiting into the lush grasses of the bald meadow. Depending on the season, you will be treated to a variety of wildflowers and blueberries that thrive along the trail and the summit.

It's important to note that the trail begins at Clingmans Dome and descends to the summit of Andrews Bald. Unlike all other hikes in this guide, most of the elevation "gain" is incurred on the return trip. Either way, this is a moderate hike with a relatively short round-trip of 3.6 miles.

View from Adrews Bald

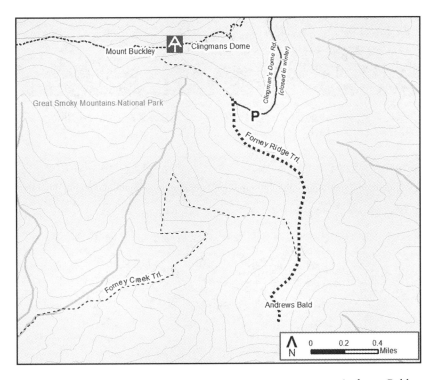

Andrews Bald

It's perfect for those wanting take a nice leg stretcher to a lovely grassy meadow with outstanding mountain views.

Artist Painting on Andrews Bald—1946. Courtesy of the Tennessee State Library and Archive

« HIGHLIGHTS

DISTANCE	»	3.6 miles round-trip
ELEVATION GAIN	»	503 feet (occurs on the return)
ELEVATION START	»	6,317 feet
DIFFICULTY	»	Moderate
HIKING TIME	»	2.5 hours
USGS QUAD	»	Clingmans Dome
MANAGED BY	»	National Park Service–Great Smoky Mountains National Park

FACILITIES AND FEES » No fees; restrooms, but no drinking water

Notes: Although the observation tower remains open all year, the road to Clingmans Dome is closed from December 1 to March 31.

Dogs are not permitted on the trails in Great Smoky Mountains National Park.

GETTING THERE »

Newfound Gap Road (U.S. 441) connects Cherokee, North Carolina, to Gatlinburg, Tennessee, within Great Smoky Mountains National Park. Take Newfound Gap Road to Clingmans Dome Road (approximately 20 miles north of Cherokee or about 16 miles south of Gatlinburg). Turn onto Clingmans Dome Road and continue 7.0 miles to the large parking area. (This road is usually closed during the winter, from December 1 to March 31. If in doubt, check the Great Smoky Mountains National Park website for road closures.)

THE TRAIL—KEY FEATURES »

0.0 MILES—The trail to Andrews Bald is actually a section of the Forney Ridge Trail. The trailhead is located to the left of the paved walkway leading to the Clingmans Dome observation tower. The sign is well marked. The trail turns to the left and begins an immediate descent through a boulder field, hugging Clingmans Dome.

0.10 MILES—There is a trail junction; the Andrews Bald trail is on the left. The trail continues to descend, entering a spruce-fir forest. You will immediately notice a striking and delightful change—the fresh scent of evergreen, the canopy of deep shade, ferns, mosses, and wildflowers.

0.5 MILES—The trail opens up briefly. You'll see a change to hardwood forest and blackberry and blueberry bushes.

0.8 MILES—The trail re-enters the lush spruce/fir environment.

1.0 MILES—There is another well-marked trail juncture. The Forney Creek Trail branches to the right. Continue straight for 0.7 miles to Andrews Bald. There is a gentle ascent for this final section.

1.7 MILES—You will break out of a shaded tunnel of deep green into an open grassy meadow sprinkled with Catawba rhododendron, blueberry bushes, and more. For expansive views of Fontana Lake and the surrounding mountains, continue down the trail for an additional 500 feet.

Reverse your route back to the Clingmans Dome parking lot.

« Gregory Bald

It's hard to find the right words to describe the beauty that awaits you at the summit of Gregory Bald without sounding ridiculously effusive. Gregory Bald is the second of two natural grassy balds in the Park being actively managed by the National Park Service. The trailhead is located in the popular Cades Cove area, nestled in the western half of the Park. At an elevation of 4,949 feet, the rounded summit rises 3,000 feet from the valley floor. Glorious, stunning, awe-inspiring—these are just some of the words that come to mind, but, in my opinion, none are able to do it justice. The 5.5-mile 3,020-foot climb from the Cove to the summit is well worth the effort. From spring through late summer, an ocean of lush mountain oat grass rolls in waves before you. The vistas will take your breath away—especially the view of Cades Cove from above, like a colorful patchwork quilt tucked into the distant valley below. However, late June provides splendor in its truest form. Numerous varieties of wild hybrid azaleas burst into bloom during this time. As you emerge from the forest and begin to absorb the garden-like meadow, the azaleas, and the vistas, you may be rendered speechless.

The author and naturalist Rose Houk describes the scene this way: "Before us bursts a fireworks show of wild azaleas in every conceivable hue—brick red, pumpkin orange, shell pink, flamboyant fuchsia, soft salmon, butter yellow, satin white" (Houk, "A Is for Azalea"). If you miss the azalea display, don't be dismayed. The vistas alone make the hike worthwhile.

The summit is also abundant with blueberry bushes, providing tasty rewards for hikers in the late summer and early fall when the berries have ripened. However, be aware that bears are likely to take advantage of nature's bounty at this time as well.

View into Cades Cove from Gregory

HISTORICAL NOTES »

Gregory's almost mystical charisma dates back to earliest times. The Cherokee called it Tsistu 'yĭ—the "rabbit place." According to the legend, numerous rabbits once made their home here. The Great Rabbit, as large as a deer, was their leader, and all the smaller rabbits were his subjects. In ancient times, people were able to see him, but not so in more recent times—that is, the late 1880's when the tale was recorded (Mooney, 407).

Gregory Bald also played a prominent role in the settlement and economy of Cades Cove. Early settlers took advantage of the lush grasses, bringing their livestock from the valley below to graze during the summer months and thus leaving valuable cropland free in the Cove. Russell Gregory, for whom the bald is named, moved to Cades Cove from Yancy

Gregory Bald

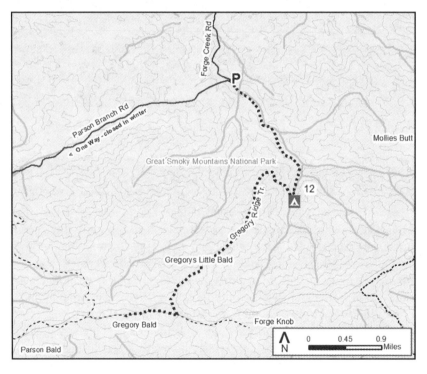

Gregory Bald

County, North Carolina, in 1835 with his wife, Elizabeth (Dunn, 44). He settled in the Cove but also loved the wilderness of the mountains and, as a rancher, took economic advantage of the high meadows. In fact, "he was famous for his method of calling cattle. Using a large blowing horn, he summoned them to the top of Gregory Bald from miles around in order to salt them" (Dunn, 44). According to historical records, he spent many hours on Gregory Bald, building a cylindrically shaped stone house with "port holes," as he called them. On moonlit nights, he would conceal himself in the house, point his rifle through a port hole, and shoot deer as they came to lick salt (Dunn, 44).

Sheep on Gregory Bald. From the Albert "Dutch" Roth Digital Photograph Collection, courtesy of Charles Roth and the Great Smoky Mountains Regional Project, University of Tennessee Libraries

Sadly, there is also a tragic story associated with the Gregory family and, by extension, the bald. The time was the 1860s, during the Civil War, a conflict that not only divided the nation but tore apart families, friends, and neighbors. Not all citizens or communities in Tennessee and North Carolina were Confederate supporters, and settlements like Cades Cove were subject to guerrilla raids. Russell Gregory, already an old man by then, was a prominent leader in the Cove and a Union sympathizer. On the other hand, Gregory's son, Charles, belonged to a band of Confederate rebels. Different stories exist regarding the exact details, but in 1864 Charles revealed the whereabouts of his father, Russell, to his band of

Confederates, and, whether he intended it or not, several members of the band forced their way into Russell's home one night and murdered him as he was rising from his bed (Dunn, 136).

The story of Russell and his son may serve as a reminder of our one of our nation's bloodiest moments in history, but today the splendor of Gregory Bald resembles nothing remotely close to violence. Although the azaleas have achieved worldwide recognition, there are rich rewards for you at any time of year. Wander throughout the meadow to see extraordinary views of Cades Cove to the north, Fontana Lake to the southeast, and Thunderhead Mountain and Clingmans Dome to the east. As a whole, this experience is one for the bucket list.

View from Gregory Bald in the Snow—1933. From the Albert "Dutch" Roth Digital Photograph Collection, courtesy of Charles Roth and the Great Smoky Mountains Regional Project, University of Tennessee Libraries

« HIGHLIGHTS

DISTANCE »	11.2 miles
ASCENT »	3,000 feet
ELEVATION START »	2,024 feet
ELEVATION END »	4,949 feet

DIFFICULTY	»	Strenuous
HIKING TIME	»	10 hours
USGS QUAD	»	Cades Cove
MANAGED BY	»	National Park Service–Great Smoky Mountains National Park
FACILITIES AND FEES	»	There are no restrooms at the trailhead, but they are available at the entrance to Cades Cove.

Note: The road to the trailhead can be accessed only via the one-way Cades Cove Loop. During the peak tourist seasons, expect heavy traffic on the loop. Also, note that from early May through September the road is closed to cars on Wednesdays and Saturdays until 10 A.M.

GETTING THERE »

From Townsend, Tennessee, take Highway 73 to the northwest entrance to Great Smoky Mountains National Park. Drive 7.5 miles west on Laurel Creek Road to reach Cades Cove. You will pass the main parking area and enter the one-way loop road. Drive to the far end of the 11-mile loop. The road makes a sharp left, but continue going straight at this junction, with the Cable Mill and Visitor's Center, and go onto the Forge Creek Road (which also leads to Parson Branch Road). Drive for another 2.2 miles to reach the Gregory Ridge trailhead. Just before you reach the parking lot, the one-way Parson Branch Road forks off to the right; continue on the two-way Forge Creek Road for a short distance to reach the Gregory Ridge Trail parking area.

THE TRAIL—KEY FEATURES »

0.0 MILES—This hike utilizes two trails—the Gregory Ridge Trail and the Gregory Bald Trail. The hike to the summit totals 5.5 miles—4.9 miles along the Gregory Ridge Trail and an additional 0.6-mile ascent on the Gregory Bald Trail.

0–2.0 MILES—This section of the trail is a gentle climb along Forge Creek through a lush understory of ferns, mosses, and wildflowers accompanied by rhododendron. At times the trail opens to a mixed hardwood forest dominated by enormous tulip poplars. You are treated to the sound of rushing water as it cascades over rocks all along the way. Wooden footbridges take you across the creek at two places. The second footbridge marks the end the second mile.

2.0–2.4 MILES—You'll cross the creek one last time. There is no bridge, and rushing water can make this crossing a little tricky. Almost immediately the trail passes a campsite (#12). At this point the trail leaves the stream behind and begins its climb in earnest.

2.4–2.9 MILES—The vegetation changes dramatically to a mix of mountain laurel and blueberry bushes.

2.9–4.9 MILES—You'll re-enter and hike through a mix of rhododendron, hardwood, and evergreen forest. You'll continue a steady climb along the ridgeline.

4.9 MILES—You'll arrive at a trail junction. The summit of Gregory Bald is now 0.6 miles to the right on the Gregory Bald Trail. You're now at an elevation of 4,605 feet.

5.5 MILES—After making the final push to the summit, you'll immediately see two paths. The left path takes you through an extensive garden of flame azaleas and blueberry bushes. Take the path to the right for outstanding views of Cades Cove. Be sure to explore the entire bald for a complete panorama of the surrounding mountains. You may see deer and a variety of birds, such as the indigo bunting, making their homes in the grasses or along the border between the meadow and forest.

Note: There is a shorter route to Gregory Bald via the Gregory Bald trail emanating from Parson's Branch Road in Cades Cove.

However, this primitive road is closed in the winter. It is also one way, so if you plan to take this route, you need to be prepared to exit the park via Parson's Branch Road.

Spence Field »

While it may not be like the others, Spence Field is indeed a grassy bald with its own unique story. Located in the Cades Cove area of Great Smoky Mountains National Park, it was in the optimal spot for the nineteenth-century settlers who used the fertile soil of Cades Cove for agriculture and the tops of the grassy balds as pastures for their livestock. Spence Field is thought to have been cleared during this time by James Spence and used as a grazing ground (Lindsay). The widespread consensus that Spence Field was in fact cleared and is not a naturally occurring bald has probably played a role in the National Park's decision to not actively maintain the bald.

Spence Field

Although trees and shrubs have invaded much of what used to be an open grassy pasture, there are still remnants of what Spence Field must have been like a century ago. Soft grass blankets the entire summit, even in places where the forest has moved in. Mountain laurel and flame azaleas have made a slow march onto the field. Fortunately, there are still pockets of open meadow that allow visitors to lie down and bask in the sunlight.

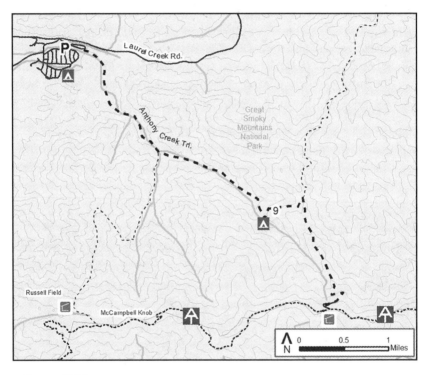

Spence Field

The charm of Spence Field itself does not undermine the beauty of the hike to get there. Although it is a thigh-burning 5.3-mile, 2,941-foot climb to the top, the hike is well worth it, as it meanders along the tumbling waters of Anthony Creek, through a lush hardwood forest, and finally through a long rhododendron tunnel on a deeply embedded cobble-stone-like trail that serves as a reminder of bygone days when livestock were herded up from the valley below.

HIGHLIGHTS »

DISTANCE	»	10.6 miles
TOTAL ASCENT	»	2,941 feet
ELEVATION START	»	2,020 feet
DIFFICULTY	»	Strenuous
HIKING TIME	»	9 hours
USGS QUAD	»	Thunderhead Mountain
MANAGED BY	»	National Park Service–Great Smoky Mountains National Park
FACILITIES AND FEES	»	No fees; restrooms, but no drinking water

GETTING THERE »

From Townsend, Tennessee, take Highway 73 to the northwest entrance to Great Smoky Mountains National Park, then drive 7.5 miles west on Laurel Creek Road to reach Cades Cove. Park at the Cades Cove picnic area at the entrance to the Cove.

THE TRAIL—KEY FEATURES »

0.0–0.30 MILES—The hike to Spence Field utilizes three well-marked trails: the Anthony Creek Trail, the Bote Mountain Trail, and the Appalachian Trail. You will begin on the 3.5-mile Anthony Creek Trail, which is located at the end of the parking lot for the Cades Cove picnic area. The trail runs along Anthony Creek. It is wide and lined with fine-cut gravel, making it easy for travelers. At about 0.2 miles into the hike you will reach a trail junction. Continue straight on the Anthony Creek

Trail. Almost immediately, you'll come upon the Anthony Creek Horse Camp.

0.30–1.6 MILES—The trail continues to meander alongside Anthony Creek, bordered by a carpet of mosses, ferns, and wildflowers. It maintains a very gentle climb for all of this segment. You will be treated to several cascading waterfalls. The trail crosses the creek by means of wooden footbridges at four places along the way. At the 1.6-mile mark, the trail splits. Continue left along the Anthony Creek Trail.

1.6–3.0 MILES—You will cross one more bridge, and then the trail becomes slightly steeper. The trail proceeds through a combination of rhododendron, wildflowers, and large tulip poplar trees. After about 3 miles you will reach Campground #9, and you are now at an elevation of 3,305 feet.

3.0–3.5 MILES—The trail leaves behind the gurgling sounds of the creek and begins a more earnest ascent up the mountain. You may catch a few glimpses of Cades Cove through openings in the trees. At 3.5 miles, the Anthony Creek Trail ends. Take a right onto the Bote Mountain Trail, and begin a 1.7-mile ascent.

3.5–5.2 MILES—The trail becomes steeper. This segment of the hike is a persistent climb. You will enter a beautiful rhododendron tunnel for a large portion of this ascent. At some points along the way, the ground level is a remarkable 5 to 6 feet above where you will be walking, giving the trail a sunken-in appearance. This is likely the result of years when livestock were herded up the trail for their summer grazing on Spence Field. At 5.2 miles you will reach the final junction. Take a right on the Appalachian Trail.

5.2–5.3 MILES—The final tenth of a mile is a time to catch your breath. Walk a short distance down the AT and you will arrive at the summit of Spence Field. Lie down in the soft grass, maybe in the shade of a tree. Although the forest has overgrown much of what used to be Spence Field, there is still plenty to see and explore, including bright flame azaleas and bright pink Catawba rhododendron in midsummer.

Roan Highlands Area

« Hump Mountain

Hump Mountain and Little Hump Mountain are located on the edge of the Roan Highlands. They are likely part of a single high-elevation prairie that once stretched unimpeded for miles across the Highlands. What remains now is a string of balds, like little caps, sprinkled across the mountain summits. These include Little Hump and Hump as well as Round Bald, Jane Bald, and Grassy Ridge Bald. Take a fascinating flight in Google Earth along this stretch of mountains lying along the Tennessee/North Carolina border. You will be amazed.

View to Hump Mountain. Courtesy of Nicholas Lenze

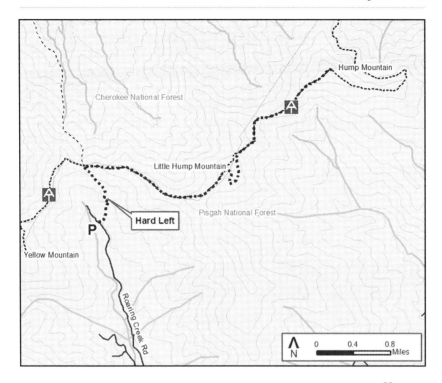

Hump

The hike to Little Hump and Hump utilizes a section of the Appalachian Trail that has been hailed by many as one of the most beautiful portions of the entire Trail. This is significant statement since the AT stretches from more than 2,000 miles Georgia to Maine. As you hike through the grassy meadows that dominate the mountainsides, you will find yourself in a world reminiscent of the Austrian Alps. Beyond the wavy yellow fields and the valleys below are undulating ranges of blue rounded peaks. Yellow coneflowers and crimson bee balm are just a few of the wildflowers that dance in the breezes during the summer months. You can actually hear the hum of bees in the meadows.

The hike described here is the longer hike to Hump Mountain. (The hike to Little Hump Mountain is also included in this guide.) Either way, just when you think it couldn't get any better, you reach that final spot, that highest point on the grassy summit where you feel at one with the world. On Hump as well as Little Hump, you have 360-degree views that simply cannot be adequately described with words. You could spend hours on either one of the grassy mountaintops, peering through binoculars, having a picnic, writing in a journal, or even just taking a nap.

« HISTORICAL NOTE

The first section of the hike utilizes a portion of the Overmountain Victory National Historic Trail. In September 1780, a group of a thousand American patriot militiamen, dubbed the Overmountain Men, left Sycamore Shoals, Tennessee, and traveled 170 miles along this route to Kings Mountain, South Carolina, where they defeated the British in a bloody battle. This historic battle freed the South from British rule and became a turning point of the Revolutionary War (National Park Service, "Overmountain Victory National Historic Trail"). A sign at Yellow Gap briefly recounts the story of the battle and the Trail. The Overmountain Victory National Historic Trail is managed by the National Park Service. For more information, you can go to http://www.National Park Service.gov/ovvi/index.htm

« HIGHLIGHTS

DISTANCE »	8.9 miles round-trip
ASCENT »	1,327 feet
ELEVATION START »	4,260 feet
DIFFICULTY »	Strenuous
HIKING TIME »	6 hours
USGS QUAD »	White Rocks Mountain
MANAGED BY »	Pisgah National Forest
FACILITIES AND FEES »	None

« GETTING THERE

The trailhead is on Roaring Creek Road off Route 19E. From Elizabethton, Tennessee, head toward Cranberry, North Carolina, on Route 19E. Once at Cranberry, continue south on 19E for just over 8 miles before turning right on Roaring Creek Road. There may not be a street sign, but there is a sign for Roaring Creek Church. Follow the road for 4.8 miles; the final section is unpaved. There will be a small parking area on the left. A locked gate is just beyond the parking area. The Overmountain Victory Trailhead is directly across the gravel road from the parking area.

From Spruce Pine, North Carolina, you can drive 15.5 miles north on Route 19E to reach the turn for Roaring Creek Road. Turn left and continue down Roaring Creek Road as described.

Open meadow and vistas along the Trail

THE TRAIL—KEY FEATURES »

0.0 MILES—You will utilize two trails for this hike—the Overmountain Victory National Historic Trail and the Appalachian Trail.

0.0–0.34 MILES—From the trailhead, follow the Overmountain Victory Trail up through a hardwood forest, maintaining a moderate climb. There is a small stream along the trail to the right. The trail, which is actually an old roadbed, is well maintained and easy on the feet.

0.34 MILES—You will come upon beautiful grassy field to the left. Although the old roadbed continues straight, you will take a 180-degree turn left into this field. This turn is very easy to miss. There is a small trail sign, but it is mostly obscured by overgrowth.

0.34–0.8 MILES—Follow the Overmountain Victory Trail across the grassy field and re-enter the hardwood forest on the other side. You will maintain a very gentle ascent through the forest all the way to Yellow Gap. As you approach Yellow Gap, the forest opens up into a wildflower-infused meadow on the right. Stay right on the trail and continue about a hundred feet to the well-marked Yellow Gap junction.

0.8 MILES—The Appalachian Trail intersects with the Overmountain Victory Trail at Yellow Gap. Take a right to go north on the Appalachian Trail, toward Little Hump.

0.8–1.46 MILES—The trail noticeably steepens after you get onto the AT. This is one of the most beautiful portions of the hike. There is a large open meadow to the right of the trail, and as you ascend, the views beyond the meadow get better and better. On a clear day, you can look behind you to the west and see the open summits of Round Bald, Jane Bald, and Grassy Ridge Bald. You can also look straight across the meadow and admire rippling blue peaks that extend as far as your eyes can see. Or, look up ahead to the right and see the large grassy cap of Big Yellow Mountain (a privately owned bald). You can even look down into the valley and see a bright red barn that has been converted into an AT shelter. The red barn, contrasting with multiple shades of green or tawny brown, makes for a lovely canvas jointly painted by humans and nature.

1.46–2.05 MILES—The Appalachian Trail leaves the meadow and re-enters the forest. You will maintain the steep climb for a bit longer before the trail begins to level off. During the summer, clusters of Turk's cap lilies and crimson bee balm decorate the trail.

2.05–2.48 MILES—You will burst out onto the open grassy crest that extends all the way to the summit of Little Hump. Embrace the on-top-of-the-world feeling as you continue through the field, toward the 5,469-foot summit. Here, you will be treated to some of the best views along the entire AT—miles and miles of blue mountain peaks, deep valleys, and endless horizon in all directions.

2.48–3.55 MILES—Continue following the AT, which makes a diagonal switchback down the other side of Little Hump. The gentle hike down alternates between open meadow and hardwood forest. Near the end of your descent you will find a campground with a water station. Your descent ends at Bradley Gap, at 3.55 miles and 4,990 feet.

13.55–4.45 MILES—This last section of the hike is a steep trek along the AT up the grassy face of Hump Mountain. The 5,587-foot summit is visible from Bradley Gap and provides continuing motivation to keep pushing to the top. Once you reach the top of Hump, you'll immediately realize that the view is worth every step of the hike. There are 360-degree views of the surrounding mountains and valleys, including the identifiable Grandfather Mountain, Little Hump Mountain, and Roan Mountain. There is a flat area to rest, have lunch, admire the views, and take a nap before heading back.

Reverse your way back down the trail to the parking area.

Note: If you continue for a couple hundred feet on the trail past the summit of Hump, you will find a plaque dedicated to Stanley Murray by the U.S. Forest Service and the Southern Appalachian Highlands Conservancy. Stanley Murray was instrumental in bringing the Appalachian Trail to this section of the mountains, and the wonderful experience that this hike offers is partly a result of his efforts.

« Little Hump Mountain

Little Hump Mountain and Hump Mountain, as noted, are likely part of a single high-elevation prairie that once stretched unimpeded for miles across the Highlands. What remains now is a string of balds that includes Little Hump Mountain and Hump Mountain, as well as Round Bald, Jane Bald, and Grassy Ridge Bald.

View up to Little Hump Mountain. Courtesy of Nicholas Lenze

The hike to Little Hump and Hump incorporates a particularly beautiful section of the Appalachian Trail. As you hike through the grassy meadows that dominate the mountainsides, you will find yourself in an alpine world of wildflowers and distant mountain peaks.

The hike to Little Hump is shorter than that to Hump. On either hike, just when you think it couldn't get any better, you reach that final spot, that highest point on the grassy summit where you feel in harmony with your surroundings. On both summits, there are stunning 360-degree views that invite you to linger and take in the beauty around you.

Stunning view on the Trail to Little Hump Mountain

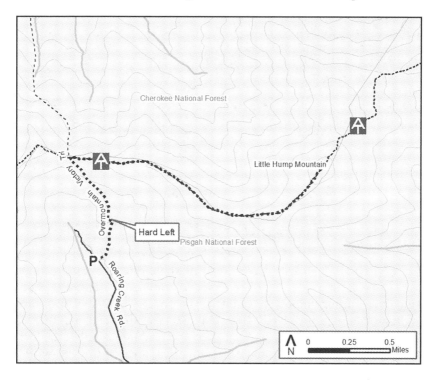

Little Hump

« HISTORICAL NOTE

The first section of the hike utilizes a portion of the Overmountain Victory National Historic Trail. In September 1780, a group of 1,000 American patriot militia men, dubbed the Overmountain Men, left Sycamore Shoals, Tennessee, and traveled 170 miles along this route to Kings Mountain, South Carolina, where they defeated the British in a bloody battle. This historic battle freed the South from British rule and became a turning point of the Revolutionary War ("Overmountain Victory National Historic Trail"). A sign at Yellow Gap briefly recounts the story of the battle and this trail. The Overmountain Victory National Historic Trail is managed by the National Park Service. For more information, you can go to: http://www.National Park Service.gov/ovvi/index.htm

« HIGHLIGHTS

DISTANCE »	5.0 miles round-trip
TOTAL ASCENT »	1,209 feet
ELEVATION START »	4,260 feet
DIFFICULTY »	Strenuous
HIKING TIME »	4 hours
USGS QUAD »	Carvers Gap, North Carolina
MANAGED BY »	Pisgah National Forest
FACILITIES AND FEES »	None

« GETTING THERE

The trailhead is on Roaring Creek Road off Route 19E. From Elizabethton, Tennessee, head toward Cranberry, North Carolina, on Route 19E. Continue south from Cranberry on 19E for just over 8 miles and then turn right on Roaring Creek Road. There may not be a street sign, but there is a sign for Roaring Creek Church. Follow the road for 4.8 miles; the final section is unpaved. You'll find a small parking area on the left, with a locked gate just beyond. The Overmountain Victory Trailhead is directly across the gravel road from the parking area.

From Spruce Pine, North Carolina, drive 15.5 miles north on Route 19E to reach the turn for Roaring Creek Road. Turn left and continue down Roaring Creek Road as described.

THE TRAIL—KEY FEATURES »

0.0 MILES—You will utilize two trails for this hike—first, the Overmountain Victory National Historic Trail and the Appalachian Trail.

0.0–.34 MILES—From the trailhead, follow the Overmountain Victory Trail up through a hardwood forest, maintaining a moderate climb. There is a small stream along the trail to the right. The trail, which is actually an old roadbed, is well maintained and easy on the feet.

0.34 MILES—You will arrive at beautiful grassy field on the left. Although the old roadbed continues straight, take a 180-degree turn left into this field. This turn is very easy to miss, because the small trail sign is mostly obscured by overgrowth.

0.34–0.8 MILES—Follow the Overmountain Victory Trail across the grassy field and re-enter the hardwood forest on the other side. Maintain a very gentle ascent through the forest all the way to Yellow Gap. As you approach Yellow Gap, you'll see a meadow full of wildflowers on your right. Stay on the trail and continue about a hundred feet to the well-marked Yellow Gap junction.

0.8 MILES—The Appalachian Trail intersects with the Overmountain Victory Trail at Yellow Gap. Take a right to go north on the Appalachian Trail, toward Little Hump.

0.8–1.46 MILES—The trail becomes markedly steeper at this point, but it is a particularly beautiful part of the hike. You'll see to your right a large open meadow, and the views continue to astound as you ascend. You can see wonderful views in all directions–the open summits of

Round Bald, Jane Bald, and Grassy Ridge Bald to the west; blue peaks straight ahead of you that go on forever; the large grassy cap of Big Yellow Mountain, a privately owned bald, to the right; below, in the vall ey, a bright red barn that has been converted into an AT shelter.

1.46–2.05 MILES—The AT leaves the meadow and re-enters forest. You'll continue the steep climb for a bit longer, but then the trail, with Turk's cap lilies and bee balm in summer, will begin to level off.

2.05–2.48 MILES—You will emerge into an open grassy crest that extends all the way to the summit of Little Hump. Continue through the field, toward the 5,469-foot summit, with some amazing views of blue mountain peaks, deep valleys, and endless horizon in all directions.

Reverse your way back down the trail to the parking area.

View at Round, Jane and Grassy Ridge

Round Bald, Jane Bald, and Grassy Ridge Bald »

The Roan Highlands have long been known for their biodiversity. The area captivated the early botanists Andre Michaux and Asa Gray and has continued to mesmerize both the scientific community and the general public. The Highlands include the largest expanse of grassy balds in the Appalachian chain as well as the world's largest natural rhododendron garden, at Roan Mountain. It's no accident that the Appalachian Trail crosses the summits of Round Bald and Jane Bald. This section of the AT boasts the highest concentration of rare plant species found along the Trail (baatany.org). The significance of these three balds is further heightened by speculation from scientists that they are "oldest [balds] in the Southern Appalachians" (Simmons).

You can experience all three balds, Round, Jane, and Grassy Ridge, with a moderate 4.9-mile round-trip hike. Each grassy summit is unique, with exceptional and ever-changing views. There is a sense of peace, openness, and freedom provided by the gently flowing grasses. At 6,200 feet, Grassy Ridge is several hundred feet higher than the other two summits, making the vistas from there even more impressive.

Fortunately, you can hike to the summit of one, two, or all three balds. Whatever you choose, you will experience something exceptional. While fall and winter in the highlands have their own special beauty, spring and summer are prime times to visit. You will see a multitude of wildflowers, including the rare Gray's lily as well as a variety of birds. You will see flame azaleas ablaze with orange clusters, and mid- to late June brings the vibrant pink/purple blooms of the Catawba rhododendron to center stage.

HISTORICAL NOTE »

Many have asked how Jane Bald got its name. Legend says that it was named for a woman named Jane who died trying to cross the bald while ill. However, in 2008 Elsie Yelton, the granddaughter of the woman who actually died shortly after she was brought down from the bald, told a different version of the story. Jane and Harriet Cook were sisters who badly wanted to visit two other sisters who lived across the mountains from them. Several times they had delayed making the trip (which required trekking across the balds) because Harriet was suffering from milk

View of Grassy Ridge Bald. Courtesy of Nicholas Lenze

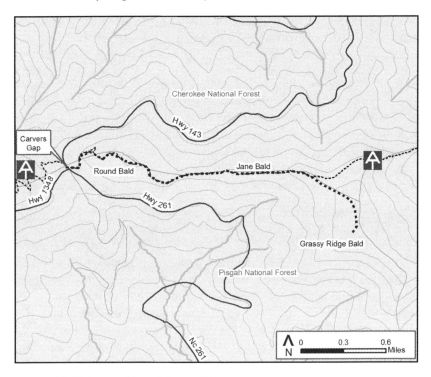

Round Bald, Jane Bald, and Grassy Ridge

sickness. Finally Harriet appeared to have recovered, so the two sisters decided to make the trip. In November 1870, they made the trip from Mitchell County, North Carolina, across the mountains to see their sisters in Carter County, Tennessee. After concluding their visit, Jane and Harriet started back. At some point, Harriet began to feel weak. The nausea and dizziness of the milk sickness returned, making it impossible for her to continue. She collapsed under a tree on the top of Jane Bald. By then, the temperature had dropped, nightfall had come, and they had no way to make a fire. They stayed together there on the bald through the night. However, at sunrise, Jane ran down to the valley to find help. She returned with a crew of men, who carried Harriet down the mountain in a wagon. Harriet died shortly after they got her home. She was only twenty-four years old. Her two-year-old son grew up to become Elsie Yelton's father. The bald on which Harriet Cook spent that fateful night now bears the name of her sister Jane (Joslin, 5–6).

Goats on June Bald—Batany Goat Project. Courtesy of Nicholas Lenze

The balds of the Roan Highlands have clearly been succumbing to forest succession. Today, the three balds are maintained via cutting, mowing, and grazing by a combination of volunteer-based efforts from the Southern Appalachian Highlands Conservancy, the Appalachian Trail

Conservancy, Friends of Roan Mountain, and the U.S. Forest Service. Examples of these efforts include the annual Grassy Ridge Mow-off, which has been held since 1995, and the Baatany Goat Project, which began in 2008 and is directed by the ecologist Jamey Donaldson and supported by Friends of Roan Mountain.

« HIGHLIGHTS

DISTANCE »	4.9 miles
ASCENT »	688 feet
ELEVATION START »	5,512 feet
DIFFICULTY »	Moderate
HIKING TIME »	3.5 hours
USGS QUAD »	Carvers Gap
MANAGED BY »	U.S. Forest Service, Appalachian Trail Conservancy, Southern Appalachian Highlands Conservancy
FACILITIES AND FEES »	Restrooms, but no drinking water; no fees

« GETTING THERE

The trailhead is at Carvers Gap on the Tennessee/North Carolina state line. Carvers Gap is located on State Route TN-143 and NC-261, a road that connects the towns of Roan Mountain, Tennessee, and Bakersville, North Carolina. You can reach Carvers Gap from Tennessee or North Carolina.

From Tennessee: From Interstate 26 at Johnson City, take exit U.S. Highway 321 to Elizabethton. Follow 321 to 19E (in Elizabethton) and turn right. Take 19E southeast to the town of Roan Mountain. Turn right on Highway 143 in Roan Mountain. Follow 143 south through Roan Mountain State Park 8 miles to Carvers Gap. The Carvers Gap parking lot is located on your right. The trailhead at Carvers Gap is *not* within Roan Mountain State Park.

From North Carolina: From Asheville take the Blue Ridge Parkway to Highway 226 North. Take 226 to Bakersville and turn north on Hwy 261/143. Take Hwy 261/143 to Carvers Gap. The Carvers Gap parking lot will be on your left.

THE TRAIL—KEY FEATURES »

0.0–.65 MILES—You will begin the hike on the Appalachian Trail. The trailhead is located on the side of the road across from the parking lot, and Round Bald is visible from the lot. The trail starts up the side of the bald and quickly enters a spruce-fir natural community. At 0.35 miles, the trail leaves the forest and enters the grassy meadow of Round Bald. The trail continues up to the 5,826-foot summit of Round Bald, where you will have spectacular views in every direction. The first section of the trail is wide and composed of well-graded gravel, making it a popular trip for visitors interested in the experience of a beautiful bald.

0.65–1.19 MILES—The trail takes a short descent down the other side of Round Bald and into Engine Gap, which separates Round from Jane. Depending on the season, this section is alive with sparkling flame azaleas and wildflowers, including the endangered, deep-crimson Gray's lily.

1.19–1.39 MILES—You next make a short ascent to the peak of Jane Bald, which, at 5,820 feet, is slightly lower than Round Bald. The trail becomes moderately steep and rocky at times. You will find that the summit is less open than the grassy expanse that capped Round Bald. Rather, it offers a different beauty, dominated in part by thickets of lush rhododendron.

1.39–1.67 MILES—The trail gently descends the other side of Jane Bald. This is a truly beautiful portion of the hike, with a brilliant display of wildflowers, blueberry bushes, rhododendron, and flame azaleas, all framed by the grassy meadow.

1.67–1.9 MILES—The trail narrows and starts to climb. This is the beginning of the ascent to the summit of Grassy

Ridge Bald, the third and final summit. At 1.9 miles there is an unmarked spur trail to the right. The AT proceeds to the left. Take the spur trail to Grassy Ridge.

1.9–2.45 MILES—The trail steepens, becoming a real climb. It is very narrow and slightly rocky for the majority of this section. You will be treated to thickets of blueberry and blackberry bushes, which spring out of the grassy carpet. Scattered among this community are the celebrated Gray's lilies and the occasional evergreen tree. A gnarled rhododendron tunnel leads you out onto the open meadow of Grassy Ridge. The trail continues through the meadow up to the 6,200-foot summit, where you may take in deep, satisfying breaths; be quick, though, because on a clear day, the views will take your breath away once again. The bald area is extensive, so take time to explore, have a picnic, or even bask in the sun on one of the large boulders. Return the way you came back to the parking lot at Carver's Gap.

Various Locations

Beauty Spot »

Beauty Spot, located in the Unaka Mountains near Erwin, Tennessee, well deserves its name. At 4,434 feet, it is a true spot of high-elevation beauty. The hike can be as short as a leisurely stroll from your car to the grassy meadow. Think picnic basket! However, Beauty Spot is also a point on the Appalachian Trail, so your hike can be extended to include a longer, more strenuous trek north to the summit of Unaka Mountain. You can also begin your hike at Indian Grave Gap and ascend 2.3 miles to Beauty Spot. The hike described here begins at the Beauty Spot parking loop with a stroll out to the summit and its stunning views; then it continues with a 1.15-mile leg-stretcher north on the AT to another grassy meadow near Deep Gap.

Beauty Spot—Amy and her dog Barkley

« HIGHLIGHTS

DISTANCE	»	2.5 miles round-trip
ASCENT	»	Minimal
ELEVATION START	»	4,434 feet
DIFFICULTY	»	Easy
HIKING TIME	»	2 hours
USGS QUAD	»	Huntdale, North Carolina
MANAGED BY	»	Appalachian Trail Conservancy–Cherokee National Forest
FACILITIES AND FEES	»	No facilities, no water, no fees

Note: For a more extensive hike, you can start on the AT at Indian Grave Gap and ascend to Beauty Spot or take the AT north to Unaka Mountain and back. The road up to Beauty Spot is a U.S. Forest Service (#230) gravel road. It is often closed in the winter.

« GETTING THERE

Take Interstate 26 to Exit 36 (Erwin, Tennessee). Turn toward Erwin at the end of the ramp onto Harris Hollow Road. At the traffic light, turn right on North Main Street (Rt. 107) and drive 0.5 mile; then turn left at the stop light onto Rock Creek Road (Rt. 395). Continue on Rock Creek Road for 6.5 miles to the Tennessee–North Carolina state line (called Indian Grave Gap). Take the gravel road to the left (there is a small parking area where you turn onto the gravel road). This is U.S. Forest Service Road #230. After 2.1 miles on the gravel road, stay to the right where the road splits, and you will arrive at the parking loop for Beauty Spot.

Note: This is a U.S. Forest Service gravel road. It can be rough and bumpy depending on time of year and road maintenance.

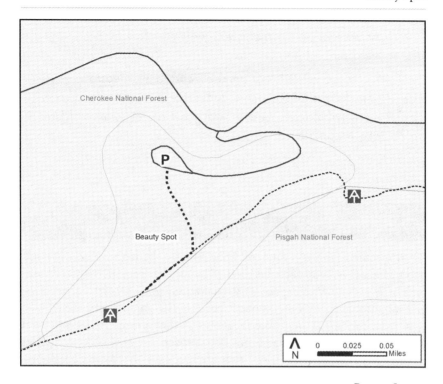

Beauty Spot

TRAIL DESCRIPTION »

0.0–0.1 MILES—From the parking area, stroll to the summit of Beauty Spot. Walk around and find the perfect spot to enjoy the views of Roan Mountain, Mount Mitchell, and other surrounding mountains.

0.1–1.15 MILES—From the parking lot, after walking out on the summit, look for metal poles painted with white blazes. These mark the Appalachian Trail. Go left (north) on the AT following the blazes and enter the mixed hardwood forest. The trail remains fairly level and is filled with ferns and wildflowers in spring and summer. You will note that the trail mirrors U.S. Forest Service Road (#230) as it continues to wind north to Unaka Mountain.

At several points along the way you can even see the road through the vegetation.

1.15 MILES—Exit the forest and descend to the meadow. Take time to wander around and have a snack. You'll see more wildflowers and a clear view of the summit of Unaka Mountain.

Reverse your route on the AT to return to Beauty Spot.

« Mount Rogers

The 8.76-mile round-trip hike to Mount Rogers, the highest natural point in Virginia, gives you the sensation of being out West, perhaps in Montana or Wyoming. It offers not only open grassy prairies, expansive views, and monolithic rocky outcroppings but also the opportunity to see wild ponies wandering through the meadows as they graze. Sometimes seen alone but more often in small herds, they present a wonderful color pallet to the eye—pintos, dusty grays, rich browns with shaggy flaxen manes, and chestnuts with shiny black manes and tails. Visiting in the spring and summer months provides the additional treat of seeing young foals scampering near their mother's sides. Introduced in 1975 to help maintain the grassy ecosystem, the ponies have become a notable attraction for the Grayson Highlands State Park, where the trailhead is located (Grayson Highlands State Park, ponies signage).

The summit, at 5,729 feet, although offering no vistas, is covered with a rich forest of Fraser fir and red spruce. It is the northernmost example of a southern spruce-fir forest in the United States (Grayson Highlands State Park, Massie Gap signage). After hiking about 3.5 miles, you will leave the open grassy meadows behind and become immersed in the dark majesty of this other world—the aroma of the Fraser fir, the verdant mosses and ferns, and the scent of the rich, moist earth.

With the prairie-like meadows, expansive vistas, wild ponies, the spruce-fir forested summit, and even the massive boulders scattered along the way, this hike is rich in variety and is a must-do!

View on the Trail to Mount Rogers. Courtesy of Nicholas Lenze

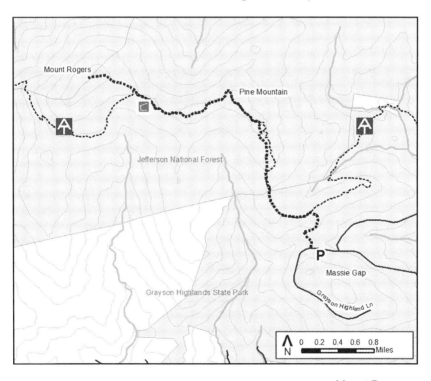

Mount Rogers

Wild ponies—Grayson Highlands State Park

« HIGHLIGHTS

DISTANCE	»	8.76 miles round-trip
ASCENT	»	1,043 feet
ELEVATION START	»	4,686 feet
DIFFICULTY	»	Strenuous
HIKING TIME	»	5.5 hours
USGS QUAD	»	Whiteside Mountain
MANAGED BY	»	Grayson Highlands State Park and Jefferson National Forest
FACILITIES AND FEES	»	Fees $4–$5. Restrooms are located along the Grayson Highland Lane, water fountains along the Grayson Highland Lane, and a water station at the Thomas Knob Shelter.

GETTING THERE »

The trailhead is located within the Grayson Highlands State Park. Depending on your travel direction, you will enter the Park from Highway 58 near the Damascus area. After entering the park, continue on Grayson Highland Lane until you reach the Massie Gap parking area. The trail begins here. What can be somewhat confusing is that the trail itself actually leaves the Park and enters the Mount Rogers National Recreation Area before reaching the summit.

THE TRAIL—KEY FEATURES »

0.0–.48 MILES—The first section of this hike utilizes the Rhododendron Gap Trail. The well-marked trailhead is located in an open field at Massie Gap and is visible from the parking lot. Follow the blue fence posts, indicating you are on the Rhododendron Gap Trail. The wide, easy trail ascends through beautiful meadows.

0.48 MILES—You will come upon a trail junction. Take a left onto the Appalachian Trail (AT) and follow the white fence posts, heading south.

0.48–1.09 MILES—Continue on the AT, which maintains a slight ascent and traverses the expansive meadow ecosystem.

1.09 MILES—You will come upon a trail junction. Although there is a sign and a map, the directions can be a little tricky. You will go through a gated fence, leaving the Grayson Highlands State Park, and enter the Mount Rogers National Recreation Area. After you pass through the gate, continue straight on the AT.

1.09–1.36 MILES—The AT becomes slightly rockier and gradually steepens. Although there are still expanses of meadow, the environment has become more enclosed by trees and shrubbery.

1.36 MILES—At 5,187 feet, there is another trail, the Wilburn Ridge Trail, forking off to the left. You have two options here. You may take a left onto the Wilburn Ridge Trail, which leads up and down the huge boulder fields of Wilburn Ridge, or you may continue straight on the AT, which maneuvers around the rocky outcroppings. Both trails are about the same distance and come together in less than a mile. The Wilburn Ridge Trail is definitely more strenuous but offers amazing views. The AT section is less difficult, and it does offer several openings for great views as well.

1.36–2.11 MILES—If you choose to take the Wilburn Ridge Trail, follow the blue-on-white marked fence posts until you rejoin the Appalachian Trail at 2.11 miles. If you choose the Appalachian Trail, continue to follow the white marked fenced posts.

2.11–2.63 MILES—Continue to hike along the AT through open meadows with exceptional long-range views.

2.63–3.89 MILES—Veer left at a marked trail junction, following the signs to stay on the Appalachian Trail. You will enter a young hardwood and evergreen forest before coming back out into the open meadow. This section is relatively flat and easy. At 3.68 miles, you will arrive at the Thomas Knob Shelter on the left. Sit at the picnic table for a rest in the shade, read the adventures of the thru-hikers written in the notebook inside, or refill your water bottles at a station behind the shelter. After this, you will continue for a short 0.2 miles to the Mount Rogers Spur Trail.

3.89–4.38 MILES—Take a right onto the Mount Rogers Spur Trail and begin the final push to the summit. You will quickly become enveloped in a mystical red spruce and Fraser fir forest. The smell of Christmas fills the fresh air as you make your way through the lush, verdant forest.

The 5,729-foot summit levels off under a shaded canopy. You can rest, inhale the crisp scent that fills the air, and enjoy a picnic lunch before heading back down for the return trip.

The Lump »

The Lump Trail is located at mile post 264.4 on the Blue Ridge Parkway northeast of Boone, North Carolina. The summit rises behind the split-rail fence at the Lump Overlook parking area. It's a wonderful place to relax, get some sun, have a picnic, and enjoy the vistas. You are treated to panoramic views of the Yadkin Valley and the Grandfather Mountain area. The trail is very short—only 0.3 miles round-trip, so a visit to the Lump can be combined with other adventures along the Parkway.

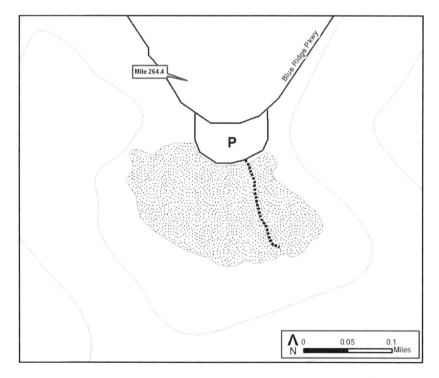

The Lump

The Lump—Legend of Tom Dula. Courtesy of Nicholas Lenze

« HISTORICAL NOTE

There is a National Park Service historical marker that highlights the tragic story of Tom Dula and his fiancée, Laura Foster, who mysteriously disappeared on the night they were to elope. Several weeks later, her body was found in a shallow grave and Tom became a suspect. He was tried, convicted, and subsequently hanged for her murder. The events occurred in neighboring Wilkes County in 1866, and the story made headlines throughout the South and as far north as New York. The legend is a classic who-done-it filled with sex, intrigue, and possibly a love triangle that included Ann Melton, Laura's married sister. The story was immortalized in the hit song *Ballad of Tom Dooley,* recorded by the Kington Trio. Much has been written about the events over the years, including a historical novel, *The Ballad of Tom Dooley,* published in 2011 by the *New York Times* best-selling author Sharyn McCrumb.

THE TRAIL—KEY FEATURES »

DISTANCE	»	0.3 miles round-trip
TOTAL ASCENT	»	None
ELEVATION START	»	3,465 feet
DIFFICULTY	»	Easy
HIKING TIME	»	15 minutes
USGS QUAD	»	Glendale Springs
MANAGED BY	»	National Park Service–Blue Ridge Parkway
FACILITIES AND FEES	»	Picnic table; no restrooms, no water, no fees

Appendix A

The Hikes Listed Alphabetically »

The Hike	Difficulty Level	Page Number
Andrews Bald	Moderate	82
Bearwallow Mountain	Moderate	41
Beauty Spot	Easy	115
Black Balsam Knob	Moderate	44
Bob Stratton Bald	Strenuous	66
Craggy Gardens from the Visitor Center	Easy	48
Gregory Bald	Strenuous	86
Hemphill Bald-Purchase Knob	Strenuous	55
Hooper Bald	Easy	70
Huckleberry Knob	Moderately Easy	74
Hump Mountain	Strenuous	98
Little Hump Mountain	Strenuous	104
Max Patch Mountain	Moderately Easy	51
Mount Rogers	Strenuous	118

The Hike	Difficulty Level	Page Number
Round, Jane and Grassy Ridge Balds	Moderate	109
Sam Knob	Moderate	62
Spence Field	Strenuous	93
The Lump	Easy	123
Whigg Meadow	Moderately Easy	78

Appendix B

The Hikes by Difficulty Level »

Difficulty Level	The Hike	Page Number
Easy	Beauty Spot	115
Easy	Craggy Gardens— from the Visitor Center	48
Easy	Hooper Bald	70
Easy	The Lump	123
Moderately Easy	Craggy Gardens— from the Picnic Area	48
Moderately Easy	Huckleberry Knob	74
Moderately Easy	Max Patch Mountain	51
Moderately Easy	Whigg Meadow	78
Moderate	Andrews Bald	82
Moderate	Bearwallow Mountain	41
Moderate	Black Balsam Knob	44
Moderate	Round, Jane, and Grassy Ridge Balds	109
Moderate	Sam Knob	62

The Hike	Difficulty Level	Page Number
Strenuous	Bob Stratton Bald	66
Strenuous	Gregory Bald	86
Strenuous	Hump Mountain	98
Strenuous	Little Hump Mountain	104
Strenuous	Purchase Knob and Hemphill Bald	55
Strenuous	Mount Rogers	118
Strenuous	Spence Field	93

Appendix C

Appalachian Trail Conservancy	http://www.appalachiantrail.org/home
Carolina Mountain Land Conservancy	http://www.Carolinamountain.org/
Cherohala Skyway	http://www.cherohala.org/
Cherokee National Forest, Tennessee	http://www.fs.usda.gov/ cherokee
Grayson Highlands State Park	http://www.dcr.virginia. gov /state-parks/graysonhighlands .shtml#general_information
Great Smoky Mountains National Park	http://www.fs.usda.gov/gwj
Jefferson National Forest, Virginia	http://www.fs.usda.gov/gwj
Leave No Trace	https://lnt.org/learn/7-principles
National Forests in NorthCarolina (for Nantahala and Pisgah)	http://www.fs.usda.gov/nfsnc
Southern Appalachian Highlands Conservancy	https://www.appalachian.org/

Bibliography

Adkins, Leonard, & Appalachian Trail Conservancy. *Images of America–Along the Appalachian Trail Georgia, North Carolina and Tennessee.* Charleston, SC: Arcadia, 2012.

Appalachian Trail Conservancy. "Hiking Safety." http://www.appalachiantrail. org/hiking/hiking-basics/health-safety (accessed March 28, 2015).

Arthur, John Preston. *Western North Carolina—A History (from 1730–1913).* Raleigh, NC: Edwards & Broughton Printing, 1914.

Baatany Project. "Baatany Project–The Goats on Roan Mountain." http://www .baatany.org/jamey.html (accessed July 7, 2013).

Bernstein, Danny. *Hiking North Carolina's Blue Ridge Mountains.* Almond: Milestone Press, 2012.

Brooks, Maurice. *The Appalachians.* Boston: Houghton Mifflin, 1965.

Carolina Mountain Land Conservancy. "Focus Areas." http://www.Carolinamountain .org/focus_areas (accessed March 28, 2015).

Carolina Mountain Land Conservancy. "Hiking Challenge—Bearwallow." http:// www.Carolinamountain.org/hikingchallenge/bearwallow (accessed March 28, 2015).

Centers for Disease Control and Prevention. "Poisonous Plants." http://www.cdc .gov/niosh/topics/plants/ (accessed March 28, 2015).

Clingman, Thomas. *Selections from the Speeches and Writings of Hon. Thomas Clingman of North Carolina.* Raleigh, NC: John Michols, Book and Job Printer,1877. http://archive.org/ (accessed March 28, 2015).

Dixon, Chris. "Appalachia's Other Trail." *New York Times,* October 5, 2007: n.p.

Documenting the American South. "Elisha Mitchell." http://docsouth.unc.edu /browse/bios/pn0001194_bio.html (accessed March 28, 2015).

Dunn, Durwood. *Cades Cove: The Life and Death of a Southern Appalachian Community, 1818–1937.* Knoxville: University of Tennessee Press, 1988.

Forest Encyclopedia Network. "Grassy Balds." http://www.forestencyclopedia.net (accessed November 17, 2011).

Forestry—Utah State University. "Forest Ecology and Succession." https://forestry .usu.edu/files/uploads/ForEcolSuccession.pdf (accessed March 28, 2015).

Gray, Asa. *Scientific Papers of Asa Gray, Vol. II: Essays; Biographical Sketches 1841– 1886.* Selected by Charles Sprague Sargent. Boston: Houghton Mifflin, 1889.

Grayson Highlands State Park, Mouth of Wilson, Virginia. Signage—Massie Gap and Ponies Great Smoky Mountains Natural History Association. *Hiking Trails of the Smokies.* Gatlinburg: Great Smoky Mountains Natural History Association, 1994.

Bibliography

Hiking the Carolinas. "Max Patch." http://hikingthecarolinas.com/max_patch .php (accessed March 28, 2015).

Houk, Rose. "'A' Is for Azalea." *Smokies Life Magazine* 3, no. 1 (2009): 10–17.

Houk, Rose. *A Natural History Guide—Great Smoky Mountains National Park.* New York: Houghton Mifflin, 1993.

Joslin, Michael. "Jane Bald—Woman Sets Record Straight on Mountain." *Friends of Roan Mountain Newsletter* 12, no. 2 (Fall 2008): 5–6.

Lanman, Charles. *Adventures in the Wilds of North America.* London: Longman, Brown, Green, and Longman, 1854. http://archive.org/ (accessed March 28, 2015).

Lindsay, M. M. *History of the Grassy Balds in Great Smoky Mountains National Park. Research/Resources Management Report No. 4.* Gatlinburg, TN: U.S. Department of Interior, National Park Service, Southeast Regional Office, Uplands Field Research Laboratory, 1976.

Lindsay, M. M., and S. P. Bratton. "Grassy Balds of the Great Smoky Mountains: Their History and Flora in Relation to Potential Management." *Environmental Management* 3 (1979): 417–30.

Lix, Courtney. "The Gift: How Great Smoky Mountains National Park Gained a Mountain." *Smokies Life Magazine* 3, no. 1 (2013): 38–45.

Mark, A. F. "The Ecology of the Southern Appalachian Grass Balds." *Ecological Monographs* 28 (1958): 293–336.

McClung, Marshall. "About Hooper Bald and Surrounding Areas." Graham County Net. http://www.grahamcounty.net/hooperbald/articles/articles.htm (accessed March 28, 2015).

McClung, Marshall. "Hooper Bald–A History." Graham County Net. http://www .grahamcounty.net (accessed March 28, 2015).

Mooney, James. *Myths of the Cherokees. Bureau of American Ethnology, 19th Annual Report.* Washington, DC: Government Printing Office, 1898.

Murray, Judy. Unpublished Interview. March 24, 2014.

National Park Service. "About Purchase Knob." http://www.National Park Service .gov/grsm/learn/nature/pk-about.htm (accessed March 28, 2015).

National Park Service. "Black Bears." http://www.National Park Service.gov /grsm/naturescience/black-bears.htm (accessed March 28, 2015).

National Park Service. "Overmountain Victory National Historic Trail." http:// www.National Park Service.gov/ovvi/index.htm (accessed March 28, 2015).

North Carolina Highway Historical Marker Program. "Judaculla Rock." http:// www.ncmarkers.com/print_marker.aspx?MarkerId=Q-4 (accessed March 28, 2015).

Pearson, S. M. "Grassy Balds." Forest Encyclopedia Network. http://www.forest encyclopedia.net/ (accessed November 17, 2011).

Saunders, Paul Richard, ed. *Status and Management of Southern Appalachian Mountain Balds: Proceedings of a Workshop Sponsored by the Southern Appalachian Research/Resource Management Cooperative (SARRMC).* Crossnore, NC: SARRMC, 1980.

Schafale, Michael P. *Guide to the Natural Communities of North Carolina, Fourth Approximation*. North Carolina Natural Heritage Program, Department of Environment and Natural Resources, 2012. http://portal.ncdenr.org/c /document_library/get_file?uuid=cbaac345-aca2–4312-acca-1004f2ba59a9& groupId=61587 (accessed March 28, 2015).

Schafale, Michael P., and David Blevins. *Wild North Carolina—Discovering Wonders of Our State's Natural Communities*. Chapel Hill: University of North Carolina Press, 2011.

Simmons, Morgan. "Grazing Goats Could Be Key to Preserving Grassy Balds." *Knoxville News*. July 30, 2008. http://www.knoxnews.com/news/local-news/ grazing-goats-could-be-key-to-preserving-grassy-ba (Accessed July 11, 2013).

Southern Appalachian Highlands Conservancy. "40th Anniversary Timeline." *View from the Highlands* 44, no. 2 (Autumn 2014):16.

Southern Appalachian Highlands Conservancy. "SAHC Focus Areas and Overview Map." https://www.google.com/maps/d/viewer?mid=zDXucNksKdiM.ktvYGq jD53HE&msa=0 (accessed March 28, 2015).

Southern Appalachian Highlands Conservancy. "SAHC's History." https://www .appalachian.org/about/history.html (accessed March 28, 2015).

Spira, Timothy. *Wildflowers and Plant Communities of the Southern Appalachian Mountains and Piedmont: A Naturalist's Guide to the Carolinas, Virginia, Tennessee, and Georgia*. Chapel Hill: University of North Carolina Press, 2011.

State Board of Agriculture. *North Carolina and Its Resources*. Raleigh, NC: M. I. & J. C. Stewart, Public Printers and Binders, 1896.

Town of Tellico Plains. "Guide to Tellico Plains—Cherohala Skyway." http://www .tellico- plains.com/cherohala-skyway.html (accessed October 11, 2016).

U.S. Fish and Wildlife Service. *Tennessee High Elevation Ecosystems*. https://www .fws.gov/asheville/pdfs/Curricula-TNhighelevation.pdf (accessed March 28, 2015).

U.S. Forest Service. "Joyce Kilmer Memorial Forest." http://www.fs.usda.gov/ recarea/nfsnc/null/recarea/?recid=48920&actid=70 (accessed March 28, 2015).

U.S. Forest Service. "Our History." http://www.fs.fed.us/learn/our-history (accessed March 28, 2015).

Warner, Charles Dudley. *On Horseback, in the Southern States*. Cambridge, MA: Riverside Press, 1888.

Weigl, Peter D., and Travis W. Knowles. "Antiquity of Southern Appalachian Grass Balds: The Role of Keystone Megaherbivores." *Proceedings of the Appalachian Biogeography Symposium*. Virginia Museum of Natural History Special Publication No. 7. 1999.

Weigl, Peter D., and Travis W. Knowles. "Megaherbivores and Southern Appalachian Grass Balds. " *Growth and Change* 26, no. 3 (1995): 365(18).

Weigl, Peter D., and Travis W. Knowles. "Temperate Mountain Grasslands: A Climate-Herbivore Hypothesis for Origins and Persistence." *Biological Reviews* (2013). Doi: 10.1111/brv.12063 (accessed March 28, 2015).

Wells, B. W. "Southern Appalachian Grass Balds." *Elisha Mitchell Science Society* 53 (1937): 1–25.

West Virginia Encyclopedia Online. "John Lederer." http://www.wvencyclopedia .org/ (accessed March 28, 2015).

White, Peter, and R. Sutter. "Managing Biodiversity in Historic Habitats: A Case History of the Southern Appalachian Grassy Balds." In *Ecosystem Management for Sustainability: Principles and Practices Illustrated by a Regional Biosphere Reserve Cooperative*. Edited by John D. Peine, 375–96. Boca Raton, FL: Lewis, 1999.

Wilderness.Net. "Joyce Kilmer–Slickrock Wilderness." http://www.wilderness .net/NWPS/wildView?WID=280 (accessed March 28, 2015).

Winegar, Deane, and Garvey Winegar. *Highroad Guide to the Virginia Mountains*, Marietta, GA: Longstreet Press, 1998.

Ziegler, Wilbur G., and Ben. S. Grosscup. *The Heart of the Alleghanies; Or, Western North Carolina: Comprising Its Topography, History, Resources, People, Narratives, Incidents, and Pictures of Travel, Adventures in Hunting and Fishing and Legends of Its Wildernesses*. Raleigh, NC: Alfred Williams, 1883. http://archive.org/ (accessed March 28, 2015).

Index

Alexander, Tom, Jr., 58
Allegheny blackberry, 23
American peregrine falcon, 25, 27
Andrews Bald, 15, 17, 40, 82–86
Appalachian bluet, 23
Appalachian gentian, 26
Appalachian Highlands Science
    Learning Center, 55–62
Appalachian National Scenic Trail. *See*
    Appalachian Trail
Appalachian Trail: history, 3, 16–18;
    hikes, 53, 99, 102, 103, 107, 109, 121,
    122
Appalachian Trail Conservancy, 17, 20,
    31, 53, 11–12, 116
Arctic bent grass, 26
azalea, 17, 23, 27, 82, 86, 90
azalea, flame, 3, 24, 39, 42, 71, 74, 92, 94,
    97, 109, 113

bald. *See* grassy bald
"Ballad of Tom Dooley," 124
Balsams, the, 21
Bataany Goat Project, 20, 109, 110, 112
bear, black, 25, 31–32, 68, 72, 87
Bearwallow Mountain, 21, 41–43
Beauty Spot, 115–18
bent avens, 26
bison, 8, 9, 11
Black Balsam Knob, 25, 44–48, 63, 64
black throated blue warbler, 25
black throated green warbler, 25
blackberry/blackberries, 17, 20, 23, 24,
    55, 81, 85, 114
black-capped chickdee, 28
Blue Ridge goldenrod, 21, 26
Blue Ridge Mountains, 10, 11

Blue Ridge Parkway, 24, 44, 47–49, 64,
    112, 123
Blue Ridge St. John's Wort, 26
blueberry/blueberries, 23–24, 39, 48, 55,
    62, 81, 82, 85, 86, 87, 92, 113, 114,
Bob Stratton Bald, 66–70
bobcat, 25
brown bat, 25

Cades Cove, 86, 87–91, 93, 95, 96
Canada warbler, 25
Carggy Knob, 48–51
Carggy Pinnacle, 48–49
Carolina Mountain Club, 53
Carolina Mountain Land Conservancy
    (CMLC), 21, 41, 42,
Carolina northern flying squirrel, 21,
    26, 27
Cataloochee Ranch, 19, 57, 58, 61
Catawba Indians, 6
Catawba rhododendron. *See*
    rhododendron
Center for Outdoor Ethics, 33–34
Cherohala Skyway, 66–81
Cherokee Indians, 4–6, 12, 15, 71, 87
Cherokee National Forest, 66, 80, 116
Cherokee, North Carolina, 85
Cherokee Removal, 15
Citico Creek Wilderness, 69.70
Civil War, 15, 89
Clingman, Thomas L.,5, 11
Clingman's Dome, 5, 82, 84–86, 90
Cloudland Hotel, 15
Cold Mountain, 55, 59
copperhead, 32
cottontail, 25
Craggy Gardens, 48–51

de Soto, Hernando, 72
Devil's Courthouse, 5, 63, 65
disjunct (species), 24, 25
diya hali yi, 6
Dula, Tom, 124
dwarf cinquefoil, 23, 24

eastern chipmunk, 25
ecotone, 16, 24, 25
edge effect, 24
elk, 9, 11, 21, 72

Ferguson cabin, 55, 58, 60, 61
filmy angelica, 23
flame azalea. *See* azalea
Fontana Lake, 82, 86, 90
forest succession, 16, 18, 111
Fork Mountain, 65
Fork Ridge, 65
Foster, Laura, 124
Fraser fir, 11, 23, 25, 26, 118, 122
Fraser, John, 11

"gant" lot, 12
Gates, W. A., 7
Gregory, Elizabeth, 89
Gilmore, Voit, 58
golden eagle, 24
golden-winged warbler, 24, 28
Grandfather Mountain, 103, 123
grassy bald: definition, 3; flora and
    fauna, 22–28; hikes, 40, 55, 57, 58,
    67, 70, 77, 78, 82, 86, 93, 109; history,
    10–21; native American legends, 4–6;
    origin theories, 7–9;
Grassy Ridge Bald, 98, 102, 104, 108,
    109–14
Graveyard Fields, 45
gray fox, 25
Gray, Asa, 11, 109
Gray's lily, 11, 26, 109, 113, 114
Grayson Highlands, 19
Grayson Highlands State Park, 118,
    120, 121

Great Smoky Mountains National Park,
    6, 14, 21, 28, 31, 34, 55–62
Great Smoky Mountains National Park,
    history, 16–18
Greenland sandwort, 26
Gregory Bald, 6, 17, 86–92
Gregory, Charles, 89
Gregory, Russell, 87–89

Heller's blazing star, 26
Hemphill Bald, 19, 55–61
Henry, Joseph, 11
highbush blackberry, 23
Hooper Bald, 13, 70–74, 78, 80
Hooper pony, 13, 71
Hooper, Enos, 13, 71
Hooper, Margaret Harbison, 71
Hooper, Marion, 13
hornet, 4, 32
Huckleberry Knob, 70, 74–77
Hump Mountain, 19, 98–104

indigo bunting, 75, 92

Jane Bald, 15, 20, 98, 102, 104, 108–14
Jefferson National Forest, 120
Joanna Bald, 6
Jonathan Valley, 58
Joyce-Kilmer Slickrock Wilderness,
    66–67, 69
Judaculla, 4, 5
Judaculla Old Fields, 4

Knowles, Travis W. , 8–11, 20

Leave No Trace, 33–34
Lederer, John, 10
Leopold, Aldo, 24
lily, Turk's cap, 48, 71, 102, 108
Little Hump Mountain, 20, 98, 99, 102,
    103, 104–8
Looking Glass Rock, 44
Lump, the, 123–25

MacKaye, Benton, 17, 69, 78, 80
magnolia warbler, 25
Max Patch Mountain, 20–21, 51–54
McNeil, Kathryn, 58
megaherbivores, 8–10
Melton, Ann, 124
Michaux, Andre, 11, 109
milk sickness, 12, 109, 111
Mitchell, Elisha, 11
Mooney, James, 4–6, 87
Moore, George, 72
Mount Cammerer, 51
Mount Mitchell, 11, 21, 59, 117
Mount Pisgah, 21, 45, 55, 59
Mount Rogers, 118–22
Mount Rogers National Recreation
    Area, 121
Mount Sterling, 51
mountain angelica, 23, 24
mountain oat grass, 22, 23, 86
mountain phlox, 23, 24
mountain sandwort, 23
mountain St. John's wort, 27
Murray, Stanley, 18, 103

Nantahala Mountains, 82
Nantahala National Forest, 66
National Park Service, 31, 49, 54, 59, 124
Native Americans, 4–8, 10, 12, 15
natural community, 9, 22, 113
Nichols, Arch, 19–20, 53
North Carolina Natural Heritage
    Program, 22
Northern saw-whet owl, 27

Oak Knob, 75, 77, 78
Odell, John, 18
Old Field, Devil's, 5
O'Neil, Kathryn, 76
Overmountain Victory National
    Historic Trail, 100, 102, 106, 109

Pardo, Juan, 72
Parsons Bald, 17

Pennsylvania sedge, 22, 23
pink shell azalea, 27
poison ivy, 33
poison oak, 33
poison sumac, 33
poloninas, East Carpathian, 9
predarmscasada inscription, 72
Purchase Knob, 55–61
pygmy salamander, 27

rattlesnake, timber, 32
raven, 24, 25
red crossbill, 25, 27
red squirrel, 25
red-breasted nuthatch, 25
relic (species), 24, 25
Revolutionary War, 100, 106
rhododendron, 5, 23, 27, 39, 48, 67, 70,
    92, 94, 96, 113, 114, 121
rhododendron, Catawba, 3, 6, 18, 21, 23,
    24, 63, 82, 109
Roan Highlands, 5, 8, 11, 14, 15, 18, 20,
    21, 109, 111
Roan Mountain, 6, 11, 13, 18, 21, 103,
    109, 112, 117
Roan Mountain bluet, 21, 27
Roan Mountain rattlesnake root, 27
Roan Mountain State Park, 112
Robbinsville, North Carolina, 6, 13, 66,
    69, 74, 76, 77
rock gnome lichen, 21, 27
Round Bald, 98, 104, 108, 109–14
Russell Field, 15, 17

SAHC. See Southern Appalachian
    Highlands Conservancy
Saltville, Virginia, 8
Sam Knob, 62–65
Sherman, Andy, 76, 78
Shining Rock, 45
Silers Bald, 17
skunk goldenrod, 24, 27
slicks, 3
snake, 32, 65

snow bunting, 25
Southern Appalachian Highlands
  Conservancy (SAHC), 18, 19, 20, 21,
  28, 58, 103, 111
southern bog lemming, 25
southern rock vole, 27
Spence Field, 15, 93–97
Spence, James, 93
spotted skunk, 25
spreading avens, 27
spruce fir moss spider, 21, 27
spruce-fir forest, 7, 22, 25, 82, 118
Stratton Bald. *See* Bob Stratton Bald
Stratton, John, 68
Stratton, Robert, 68
strawberry, wild, 23, 24
Strother, John, 10
Swag Country Inn, 57, 61, 63

Tanasee Bald, 4, 5
Tennet Mountain, 45
three-toothed cinquefoil, 23, 24
Thunderbolt Knob, 58, 61
Thunderhead, 17, 90, 95

Trail of Tears, 12
trillium, 42
Tsistu ꞌyĭ "Rabbit Place," 6, 87
Tsul ꞌkălû, 5

ulagu, 4
Unicoi Mountains, 13, 67, 70, 75, 78

vesper sparrow, 28
Virginia big-eared bat, 28

Warner, Charles Dudley, 13
wavy hair grass, 23
Weigl, Peter, 8–11, 20
Wells, B. W., 7–8
Whigg Meadow, 78–81
Whiting Manufacturing Company,
  72
whorled loosestrife, 23
woodland jumping mice, 25
wretched sedge, 27

Yadkin Valley, 123
yellow jacket, 32–33